G000094493

YOU DON'T LOOK THAT OLD!

This edition published in Great Britain in 2011 by Prion Books
an imprint of the Carlton Publishing Group
20 Mortimer Street
London W1T 3JW

A catalogue record for this book is available from the British Library

ISBN 978-1-85375-829-4

Printed in China

10 9 8 7 6 5 4 3 2 1

First published in Sweden as *Du ser inte så gammal ut!* in 2004

YOU DON'T LOOK THAT OLD!

The Hilarious Truth About Ageing

RICKARD FUCHS

Translated by Laurie Thompson

PRION

Contents

Signs of
Ageing

There are many indications to suggest that you are growing a bit older.

The trick is to learn not to recognize them.

But that's not as straightforward as it sounds: most people do recognize a grey hair when they see one.

Grey hair is often associated with approaching senility, and when you discover your first grey hair, all kinds of reaction can ensue, depending on what kind of person you are. If you are dramatically inclined: "My God! A grey hair! Now I'm ancient."

If you are very dramatically inclined: "What is that I see before me? No, no! It can't be… A grey hair! All is lost!"

If you are a disciple of renunciation: "Oh, look, a hair that seems to be a bit on the grey side. It can't be one of mine."

Grey hair belongs to the group of visible signs of ageing. Other indicators are wrinkles (or laugh-lines, as they are also called in a desperate attempt to isolate them from the ageing process), flaccid skin, cellulite, little bags here and there, in your face and elsewhere on your body, and brown spots and patches that weren't there before. All these physical signs of ageing are more or less clearly visible, whether you like it or not.

You often sleep less well as the years go by, which makes you look tired and the little bags under your eyes are emphasised as a result. One fine day you stand in front of the mirror and stare incredulously at what you see. If your luck is out, the lighting will be strong and bright, and all of a sudden you will see things you have never seen before and would prefer not to see.

"My God, what a mess I look! I have lots of wrinkles all round my eyes! And not only there – my face is full of wrinkles. And just look at my hair, dry and limp. And grey! There's a grey hair, and there's another. I'll soon be completely grey-haired, and I'll look like Grandma, for God's sake. Have I had bags under my eyes as big as these before? They're not ordinary bags, they look like Woolworth's carrier bags; when did I get them? And that brown patch on my hand, was that there before? And there's another brown patch. Where do they all come from? Brown patches like that show that you're old. But I can no doubt scratch them away with my finger, they must come from that chocolate I've just eaten. Ow, that hurts when I rub them, could it be rheumatism? My grandma had rheumatism when she was old. Or was it gall stones? No, it was rheumatism, I think. And her hair was completely grey. My God, but I look old: wrinkled and baggy and grey-haired. It's lucky that the patches on my hands were only chocolate stains."

And there are other tell-tale age give-aways as well. What do people of different ages have in their wallets or handbags, for instance? When you're a certain age they contain condoms, platinum cards giving VIP access to dodgy nightclubs, and a bundle of banknotes. People of a different age might have photographs of their children, shopping lists and little notes with messages from the day nursery staff. And the wallets and handbags of another age group might well contain photographs of their grandchildren, carefully inserted into the pocket that also contains their senior rail card.

All you need do is to take a quick look in the refrigerator if you want to establish the age of the owner. If it contains a half-bottle of vodka, a lump of cheddar looking blue rather than yellow, a jar of olives and a red stocking, it is likely that the age of the owner is different from the person whose fridge contains yogurt, Xyloproct, soda water and Flora Proaktiv margarine.

When you are twenty-five you can party all night, work all the next day and then play tennis for a couple of hours in the evening when you come home from work. When you are forty, you spend half the night partying, feel a bit tired at work the next morning but still have enough energy to play tennis for almost an hour in the evening. At the age of sixty you leave the party well before midnight, feel exhausted the next morning and spend the evening watching tennis on the television. When you are eighty you go to bed before it gets dark, feel tired all the next day and shortly before dinner you fall over your old tennis racket and break your hip.

It is not only your energy that decreases with advancing age: so does your enthusiasm. The unbridled youthful enthusiasm that bubbles over in a thirty-year-old has generally turned into an almost entirely extinct volcano in a sixty-year-old. When you are younger you soon become keen and committed. The flame burns brighter when you are young. You throw yourself into things you feel strongly about with

unlimited gusto. You do voluntary work and are active in several altruistic organisations and support worthy causes. You distribute pamphlets on behalf of the societies "Homosexual Whales Against Racism" and "Down With Everything But Up With Some Things."

When you are young you react much more strongly to ideas and proposals. If somebody suggests something you approve of, you shout: "Good idea! Wicked! Let's do it! Let's get going right away!" When you are a little older, the same suggestion is greeted with: "Hmm. Well, perhaps it might be a possibility. But it sounds a bit problematic, don't you think? I really don't know. Have you asked anybody else?"

A lot that seems obvious when you are young seems to be less straightforward when you are elderly. What is so self-evidently black or white when you are young has a tendency to turn into various shades of grey when you are a little older. References and values change, as does taste. It may not always be possible to say that a person's taste gets better or worse – who is qualified to be a judge of that? – but very often tastes do change as time goes by. That film you saw when you were twenty and thought was fantastically good, for instance, is not nearly so good when you see it at the age of forty. Why is that? Is it the film that has changed? If so, how was that done? But it was so incredibly good when you saw it twenty years previously. When you watch it now, you think: how on earth could I have thought that this was any good? The actors have muscles instead of talent, and the awful script has replaced plot with explosions. An hour and forty minutes filled with bigger biceps and more bomb blasts than

any normal person ever wants to see. The hero occasionally gapes at the camera and says something stupid. Then he flexes his muscles and three motor cars explode. And I used to think that was good.

Our conception of entertainment also changes. The longing to attend deafening rock concerts might be replaced by a later desire to watch musicals, funnyish revues or stereotype farces where everybody runs in and out of various doors losing their composure and their trousers. At various times in life we might prefer night clubs, pornography clubs, bridge clubs or early-afternoon bingo. Literary taste usually embarks on an odyssey as well. From comics (where some disembark for good), via juvenile books to "adult literature". At some point in middle age novels usually tend to be replaced at least in part by memoirs and biographies (such as the classic bestseller *My Brother Was an Only Child*).

Do we become more serious-minded when we grow older? It often seems so. The ageing process seems to bring with it more thinking and more reflecting on life. This, and perhaps also the blows life hands out to most of us, leads to less irresponsibility and more seriousness. Does that mean we become more boring? Sometimes. Our declining enthusiasm can doubtless also make us appear to be more boring than when we were young. Do we become grumpier as time passes? This is very individual. Some people who are dissatisfied with their life and think it hasn't turned out as they would have liked naturally become grumpier. Others might think that life is just great and their *joie de*

vivre increases rather than decreasing. By the time they reach eighty-eight they are totally euphoric and climb up the wall with joy. (Or in their attempts to break out of their long-term care ward.)

Aggression usually decreases as you grow older. That is probably to do at least in part with the production of less testosterone in your body. But that doesn't prevent you from flying into an occasional fury. Especially when you think about how old you are.

You might well ask if desperation is a sign of ageing. Middle-aged men (and also women, to a lesser extent) sometimes try to rediscover their youth by taking a new and significantly younger partner. Does it help? Does that make you any younger? Is it possible to keep desperation and the fear of getting old at bay by being together with somebody much younger than you are? Isn't it more likely to remind you of your age every time you see your partner's apple-red cheeks and smooth skin, and notice how easy it is for your partner to move? No doubt different people react in different ways, but it does seem clear that many people think they have grown younger if their partner is the same age as their children. Or, if you are sufficiently rich and famous, your grandchildren.

In their never-ending endeavours to rejuvenate themselves, some men buy a large motor cycle. Now they will be young again! According to Einstein's theories, we can travel backwards in time if we go quickly enough, preferably faster than the speed of light. For that you need a 1200cc model painted bright red. Pile on the horse power, and off we go! Now we'll be young again! Grey hair fluttering in the wind, facial wrinkles flattened out by the slipstream, and every inch of the body tensed in youthful hubris. It's possible that a big, fast motorbike won't make you any younger, but it's a good way of reducing the odds against having to grow any older.

How old do you have to be before you start going on about how "you have to make the most of your time" and "carpe diem" and "you never know what the future holds in store…"? When a certain age is reached, these sentences start cropping up in conversations with contemporaries.

"You have to live in the here and now, you never know what's round the corner."

"Well said! You've got to make the most of life now. Now! Tomorrow might be too late."

"Yes. Or the day after tomorrow. I'm going to the theatre tomorrow."

These Doomsday conversations are often sparked off when somebody in your circle has been struck down with a serious illness,

or died. You are reminded of the transience of life, and the fact that everything hangs by a thin thread. Best to make the most of things before it snaps.

"You have to live every day as if it were your last! You have to make the most of every day, and do exactly what you want to do!"

"That's not possible, I'm married."

How Old
Are You?

How old are you?

Twenty? Thirty? Forty? Fifty? Sixty? Seventy? Eighty? You don't know?

Can you read this page without glasses?

Can you read it with glasses?

Have you forgotten where you left your glasses?

Have you forgotten if you wear glasses?

Do you sometimes feel that you have passed your best-before date? Do you feel like a forgotten carton of milk on the bottom shelf of the fridge, or a lump of liver pate right at the back slowly taking on an unpleasant greenish hue? Do you think you have reached the age when there is a risk of your birthday cake collapsing under the weight of all the candles? (And you can't blow them out as you are driven back by the heat.) Do you need more than three matches to light all the candles on the cake? If so, is it because the matches are unusually short? If not, what *is* the reason? Do you feel it's a good thing that your birthday falls in the winter, because your birthday cake heats up the whole house?

When people tell you: "You look so young!", you know that you are not young any longer. Nobody says that to young people. It's the same kind of thing as saying to somebody who is or has just been ill: "My, you look well!" We all need cheering up a bit.

18

"My, you look so young!"

Compared with what? The Egyptian pyramids?

When do you get old? In your own eyes? In other's eyes? (Truth is in the eye of the beholder. Unfortunately.) How do you know that you are old? Is it something you can decide for yourself, or is it the world around you that decides for you? Should our friends tell us when we're old? Or is it our enemies who do that? Is it our children who tell us we can be considered elderly? Or our grandchildren? Or our great-grandchildren? (If you have great-grandchildren the odds are you don't need anybody to tell you that you're getting on a bit.}

Like so much else in life, age is relative. When you're twenty-eight, some nice little kid might say: "Excuse me, can you tell me the time, please?", or perhaps: "Hand over that watch or I'll beat you up!" (depending on what type of nice little kid it is). In both cases you feel unnecessarily old. Or perhaps you are fifty-six and an eighty-year-old says to you: "Now then, young fellow, have one of these sweets," or perhaps: "Hand over that watch, you young bastard, or I'll beat you up!" (depending on how big the eighty-year-old's pension is and how wisely he's invested it).

All things are relative, and there aren't any rules for when you are old, young, getting on a bit, elderly, etc.

Instead of asking yourself how old you are, you can ask: How old do I feel? After all, you are no older than you feel. (Always assuming you feel quite old.) The problem is that you feel differently on different days, One day you're young and vital, brimming over with enthusiasm and the sheer joy of living; the next day you feel as if you need permission from the fire brigade before lighting the candles on your birthday cake.

Sometimes there can be a big difference between how old you feel and how old you really are, or how old you look. Do you get any younger because you feel younger? Or do you just make a fool of yourself and appear even more pathetic by behaving and dressing like somebody younger? Is it OK and socially acceptable to be a forty-two-year-old teenager? Clothes and musical tastes are one thing, but should you really have a partner aged sixteen? Should you postpone the pleasures of old age until you are considerably older, and become forty-two when you're seventy-five instead? Buy a Porsche and chase after young girls aged thirty-five? Something to look forward to.

But you grow older all the time. (All being well). If you should ever doubt this fact, all you need to do is to dig out some old photographs of yourself. These old snaps not only confirm beyond all doubt that time passes, they are both entertaining and depressing at the same time. You nearly always look so young in these photographs, and so... ridiculous. But young. Fancy hair styles and lots of hair – where's it all gone? – ludicrous clothes (how on earth could I wear anything like that?!) and bright eyes brimming over with illusions (compare them with the eyes that appeared in the mirror this morning). These pictures really do make you happy and sad.

Somebody once said that the secret of eternal youth is lying about your age. This is a very doubtful claim and not a sure way of getting to the source of youth. It can be hard to say that you are twenty-three if you look as if you are forty-six, and it's not easy to maintain that you are twenty-eight if you look as if you are seventeen (i.e. fifty-six).

"How old are you?"

"I'm approaching forty."

"Really? From which direction?"

It can be hard to accept the fact that you are a bit older than you imagine you are. Reality and your passport photo are not really in step with your feelings and your understanding of the situation. Surely I can't be that old, you tell yourself, put out and a bit annoyed. Then you look at yourself in the hall mirror and see a stranger, considerably older than you are, and you stare back at the image with a raised eyebrow. Who's that?

When you are young you pull faces into the mirror.

When you are middle-aged the mirror gets its own back.

We don't always notice the tooth of time gnawing away discreetly at us. It's easier to see it in others. "I met Christine the other day. My goodness, she does look old!" And Christine goes home and says: "I bumped into Margaret the other day. Goodness me, but she does look old!" Not to mention all those school reunions where you meet your former classmates and are shocked by how old they look. Looking at them really does impress upon you how time has gone by, and it wasn't only yesterday that you were playing ball with them in the school yard. When the party's over you go back home to your husband or wife and say: "They'd all become so old that they didn't recognize me!"

That's a sentence to chew over.

It's surprising how many people of our age are so much older than we are. Can it have something to do with the water? We often want to believe that we're a bit younger than we really are. And we'd very much like other people to think that as well. So what do people mean when they say: "I don't know how old you are, but you look much younger!"?

Another sentence to chew over.

Spontaneity
and
Impulsivness

Generally speaking, you get less spontaneous and impulsive as you grow older. Bit by bit your spontaneous ideas and impulsive inspirations fade away as your birthdays mount up like beads on a necklace. It is unusual to come across people beyond the age of fifty who react spontaneously or impulsively. There might be good sides and bad sides to the fact that these qualities deteriorate as you grow older. You no longer rush off and do silly things without a second thought simply because you are a bit older now; but there again, you might be letting life pass you by. When you're young, there is often no difference between what you think and what you do. Not infrequently the action comes before the thought, or at least before the afterthought, and that can sometimes be a bit on the awkward side.

Spontaneous and impulsive outbursts such as: "Let's jump in headfirst!" or "Let's go to India for a year!", or perhaps, after knowing somebody for four hours, "Let's get married!" can have unexpected and not always desirable consequences. It is not a good idea to jump in headfirst if you don't know how deep it is. (This applies to both the literal and the metaphorical meaning of the phrase). Going to India can no doubt be a pleasant experience, but if you are thinking of staying for a year, a certain amount of planning and reflection is called for. Getting married is generally quite a big step to take, and if you are going to do it after having known each other for four hours, it becomes an even bigger step. Especially if both parties have been very drunk for those four hours and their only known mutual interest is a need for immediate gratification.

Other impulsive suggestions made with the carefree enthusiasm of youth might be: "Let's go to the bull running in Pamplona tonight!" (The outcome is a four-week stay in a Spanish hospital and a lifelong hatred of cattle).

A frequent spontaneous thought or proposal is: "Let's risk it!" This can refer to running over a level crossing before the approaching train gets there, or not using a condom. In both cases the outcome could be life-threatening.

It is also easier to be financially irresponsible when you are younger and give way to impulsiveness. The casino is an excellent place to be impulsive in when you're on holiday. "Let's stake the whole of our holiday money on red! I have the feeling it's going to be red. Red, red, red! – Black. Ah well, I expect the Consulate will pay for us to get back home."

It might often seem to be a good idea to give in to financial impulsiveness on many occasions. "What an absolutely divine wristwatch! I'll buy it. It's far too expensive of course, but I must have it. There'll no doubt be some way of paying the rent and buying food."

Certain kinds of financial irresponsibility occur no matter what your age. "Let's invest all our savings in Ericsson shares!" But it's probably only young people who resign their jobs to spend three years sailing round the world, or because they rather fancy becoming a sheep farmer, despite the fact that the nearest they've ever been to a sheep was when they were served with a lamb chop and potato gratin at Auntie Betty's. Moreover, only young people dash into a tattooist's that

is open until late at night shouting: "We want to be tattooed! We want each other's name and a rose on our bottoms! What did you say your name was?"

It is possible to erase a tattoo, which can be a good thing to know rather sooner than you might think if you find a new partner.

"Why does it say Constance on your right buttock?"

"Does it? Er... I don't know."

"What do you mean, you don't know? My name's Emily."

"Yes, well... I've no idea how it got there. Somebody must have written it there when I wasn't looking."

Not only are you more impulsive when you are younger, you are also more daring. It is not easy to say if this is because you are more naïve when you are younger, or if you are bolder. Or is it because you are less cautious? Less knowledgeable? More stupid? Whatever the reason, you are bold enough to give way to your spontaneous reactions more frequently. When you are a bit older, you tend to think first and refrain later. You also become more cautious and comfortable as the years go by, which are also reasons why you prefer to stand back. "Yes, well, I expect it would be great fun to do that, but it seems a bit of an effort." If the spontaneous proposals referred to earlier in this chapter were to crop up when you are

older, you would not commit yourself without a moment's thought. There would be all kinds of reasons and arguments for holding back.

"Let's jump in headfirst!"

"Steady on, not right now, I've only just finished eating. You shouldn't bathe on a full stomach. How deep is it here? Is the water cold? Is there any seaweed here? I hope the bottom isn't all muddy." No chance of jumping in headfirst here, oh no.

"Let's go to India for a year!"

"India? What on earth would we do there? How would we be able to provide for ourselves in India? Who would water the houseplants while we're away? Don't you need to be vaccinated before going to India? Besides, I saw in a television programme that India is swarming with snakes. Can you have anti-snake jabs? And it's so easy to get gastric problems in India. Eric and Susan went to an Indian restaurant in Birmingham and they got terrible stomach upsets. I think they had one of those red chickens."

No trip to India, then.

"Let's get married!"

"Married? To each other, you mean? Now let's not rush things. It's a big step to take. And we'd need to do something about a premarital

settlement. This is something to be approached slowly and carefully. It's probably best to sleep on it for a month or two."

"Let's go to the running of the bulls in Pamplona tonight!"

"Pamplona? Bulls? I don't know about that – I have a touch of back ache. And Pamplona, that's in Spain, isn't it? I'm not too fond of Spanish wines. And it's a bit expensive getting there. Besides, I have a pain in my foot."

When you are a bit older, the answer to all kinds of possible and impossible proposals is often: "No, I'm too old for that" or "It sounds like a bit of an effort. It's probably as well to give it a moment or two's thought. And then say no."

Or: "I'm tired. And a bit allergic. I expect it would be too expensive as well, we can't afford that kind of money. No point in throwing your savings away. It sounds a bit of an effort. Did I mention that I'm tired as well?"

"Thus the native hue of resolution is sicklied o'er with the pale cast of thought", wrote Shakespeare. One wonders how old he was when he wrote that.

There are three signs that show you are growing old:
  1. You forget things.
  2. Er... I've forgotten the other two.

The above quotation (by a 32-year-old) does not correspond to reality. All people forget things, irrespective of age. It certainly true that old people are more likely to forget things, but young people forget as well. However, forgetfulness is often the must usual reason why you start wondering if you have grown a little older than you were the other day.

"Where did I put the car keys? I had them a moment ago. Where are they? I must be getting old, dammit. Oh, there they are, on the kitchen table. That must mean I'm not that old after all."

It's not so strange that we forget things, no matter how old we are. All the time we find ourselves with more and more things to attend to and remember about. Entry code number, ATM numbers, pin numbers, the name and telephone numbers of people we barely know. Increasing stress also makes us more distrait and unfocused, which in turn makes us forget things. When we forget something, we grow more stressed than we were before, which makes us forget things still more easily. In the end we sound like a parody.

"Did you see that film on the box the other night, terrific, with that handsome bloke, what's his name, er, he's *so* famous, what's he called, he was in that film with her, what's her name, marvellous film, it's called something to do with love, I think, no, that was a different film, never mind, that tall bloke was in it as well, you know the one I mean, he's *so* famous, what the hell's he called, he used to be married to that woman who was in a TV series, I've forgotten what it's called, what's her name, fair haired, they got divorced later, did you see that film on the box, last Thursday I think it was?"

We sometimes forget what we were going to say halfway through a sentence. Then we remember, say three words and then forget again. That's because we have so much in our heads at the same time that there's not enough room for all our thoughts. Our thoughts flutter around inside our heads, collide with one another, pick themselves up, then dash off again, sometimes in the wrong direction.. We go into a room and say: "What was I going to do here?" We go back to the room we've just come from to collect our thoughts, whereupon we immediately forget that we were really going to go to the other room and do something. This has nothing to do with our age, of course, but is due to the rooms being at an angle.

If we start to think that we're beginning to get more forgetful because of increasing age, we like to reject any such suggestion. "I have a

photographic memory. It's just that I sometimes forget to remove the lens cover."

When people who are significantly younger than we are start to complain about forgetting things, we feel pleased and reassured. We tell ourselves that we don't need to remember everything, and there are more important things in life than having a good memory. We joke about it and say: "I have an extremely good memory, but it's short." We also maintain that it is not at all self-evident that it's always an advantage to remember everything. "My wife has a terrible memory. She never forgets anything."

When we think we are forgetting rather more than is desirable, we start writing things down on scraps of paper. Then we forget where we've put the scraps of paper. Or we don't understand what it says on them. We've forgotten what the telegram-style messages mean. "It says here 'Ellen Monday'. What's that supposed to mean? Ellen Who? Which Monday? Eh? And underneath it says 'not'. What the hell does that mean? Not Ellen? Not Monday? What not? When did I write this? I don't remember writing this. The bit of paper was in my brown suit – I haven't worn that for weeks. What if it's something important? Who the hell is Ellen?

Even if we do in fact grow more forgetful as we get older, most of us can handle it. But there are people who find forgetfulness a bit more problematic than others. Certain professions are affected more than others by the usual everyday sort of forgetfulness. Pilots, for instance. "What's that little green needle indicating? Huh, I've always known what it meant, it's so annoying when you forget. Is it the altimeter? No, it can't be. It's something important, I do remember that. And what's that red light flashing on and off there? I don't think it usually flashes. Ah well, my memory's not what it was."

Acting is a profession for which a memory in good working order is essential. It's not funny to find yourself standing on stage when you've forgotten your lines. The audience gaze expectantly at the poor actor, who has no idea what to say. It sometimes happens that actors in a situation like that start reciting lines from a quite different play. Unless they are in a modern, avant-garde play where anything at all can happen, the audience might well be somewhat confused. In a modern, light-hearted farce it sounds a little odd if the leading man suddenly says: "Oh mighty Caesar, dost thou lie so low?" And their bewilderment is not eased if the leading lady sticks to the script and replies: "Good grief, Jimmy, have you lost your trousers yet again?"

Doctors can also have problems when stress or old age or a combination of both starts to affect their memories, especially if the man concerned is a surgeon and conducting an operation. "Let's see, how are you supposed to make the incision in a case like this? I've done it lots of times before. It's so embarrassing to have to ask. Afterwards everybody keeps going on about how you're starting to grow old, or cracking jokes about having a bad memory. I really don't want to summon another surgeon. I'll take a bit of a chance. I think you're supposed to do it like this. Oh dear. Oh dear, oh dear, oh dear."

Food

A person's relationship with food and eating habits change with increasing age. When you are young you are often more of a gourmand (you eat a lot) than a gourmet (you eat well). When you are in your twenties it's more important to eat large portions than to partake of epicurean French cuisine. (This applies more to men than to women.) When you grow a little older, the acme of the culinary art is no longer a 400-gramme hamburger or a 800-gramme T-bone steak – both of them accompanied by colossal portions of chips. As you grow older your taste in food changes and becomes more subtle. What you like best also changes as the years go by. The young meat-eaters often turn into rather older fish-eaters. The T-bone is replaced by fish bones.

When you are a little older, you also grow more conscious of what you ought to eat from a health point of view. You don't worry about such matters when you're young. Then, you shovel into your mouth anything that crosses your path. Bloody steaks with Béarnaise sauce and chips, fried pork with onion sauce, chocolate cake with whipped cream. Round about the beginning of middle age (whenever that is), you become conscious of the fact that not all food is equally healthy. The mass media bombard us constantly with the latest terrifying results of nutritional research. Placards and headlines blare out what we must on no account eat if we want to see the end of the year. You ignore all this when you are young, but as you grow a bit older you read all the articles with trembling hands. Fat, biscuits and sausages can kill. We can eat white fish, black pudding and fried potatoes

once a week provided we promise to sick it all up as soon as we've swallowed it. Thick sauces, fast-food carbohydrates and slow-fried lamb chops are allowed only at our birthday parties, provided we skip the cake. All these warnings and recommendations are enough to ruin anybody's appetite.

Whenever we sit down to eat, if we have to think about cholesterol, sugar levels, arteriosclerosis and heart attacks, it's no wonder that eating tends to lose its appeal. It's not possible to enjoy the delicious sauce while seeing before your very eyes the newspaper headline "Sauce Kills!" It's not uplifting to sink your teeth into a newly grilled beef steak and simultaneously see in your mind's eye (it's just behind your nose) the placard: "Dig a grill, dig a grave!" The meat seems to swell in your mouth and threaten to choke you, and it doesn't taste nearly as good any longer. And if you are rash enough to have a sauce with your grill, you can rest assured that you are doomed. Finished. End of story. Sauce kills and grilled beef will dig your grave. All you need to round things off is a Hot Cross Bun and Angel Delight.

Eating is no fun if everything you ingest casts a doom-laden shadow of ill-health before it. Obviously, especially when we are no longer twenty, we should try to eat food that is more or less good for us, but we shouldn't go overboard on this. If everybody were to eat what's

good for you and "the right stuff", who could guarantee that we would all have a long and healthy life? And even if such guarantees were forthcoming, is that really how we'd like things to be? Would we really want to live a few years longer if all we could eat was sultana bran, figs and minced hardboard (contains a lot of fibre)? No chocolate, no Danish pastries, no sauces, no butter, no cheese, no cream cakes, veal fillets or Black Forest gateau. Eat only what's good for you. Then you'll have the pleasure of dying as fit as a fiddle. (Unless you've fiddled a bit on the way.)

As you grow older, you often find that the amount and the kind of food you can eat changes. Your digestive system changes, and you can no longer devour anything going and portions as big as they come. Sometimes your gall bladder makes its presence felt, at others your stomach refuses to co-operate. You discover what you can eat and what you can't eat. As you grow older, your interest in cooking tends to increase. (This applies more to men – women are often more interested in cooking from an early age.) All of a sudden the head of the household, who has never before displayed the slightest interest in culinary matters and has had considerable difficulties in boiling an egg, announces his intention of preparing a Queue de beuf Dauphinoise with glazed chestnuts. Afterwards the kitchen looks like a bomb site and the whole family goes to McDonald's.

Even what you order in a restaurant changes as the years pass by. When you are young, the price and the size of the portion tend to be more significant than when you are older. You want something else instead of a pizza, and rather than an entrecôte, you go for grilled turbot. Those yummy desserts that contain eight thousand calories and hence have been featured in the press under the headline: "Deadly Desserts! We Reveal The Whole List!", are quietly dropped and replaced by a small plate of yogurt-lite containing three blueberries. It's not as tasty as chocolate cake with vanilla ice cream and whipped cream, but it satisfies the need we feel as we grow older to eat what is "good for us". Our stomachs and cholesterol levels might well benefit as a result: whether or not we do is another matter.

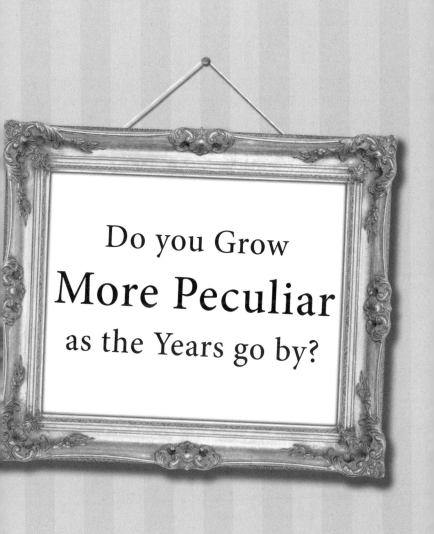

Do you Grow
More Peculiar
as the Years go by?

It is almost inevitable that you change as the years go by.

Do you become more peculiar?

Or is it the other way round – do you tend to become more normal if you were a bit odd previously? Certain traits of character become more pronounced as you grow older. Aspects of your personality which were barely noticeable or not noticeable at all when you were younger blossom forth as you approach middle age. What used to be small eccentric blemishes that nobody paid any attention to become distinct oddities as the years pass. The barely noticeable thriftiness Bruce displayed in his twenties has become "he's extremely tight-fisted" in his thirties, and by the time Bruce reaches the age of fifty his parsimony is full-blown. He even starts wearing shoes that are too small for him so that he can make use of the packet of corn plasters he was given for nothing.

People who are a little on the pessimistic side in their youth often become prophets of doom when they grow older. In their eyes everything is dismal and cheerless, and most things will probably go to the dogs. As far as they are concerned the pinkest of clouds with rims of gold are dark grey thunderclouds.

"We're going to Thailand for our holidays."

"Lucky you! Sun and swimming in the sea every day!"

"I don't think so. It's bound to be pouring down."

"It never rains there at this time of year."

"There's always a first time."

"No, no, I promise you it won't rain at this time of year."

"Then I expect we'll get sun-stroke."

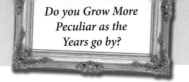

*Do you Grow More
Peculiar as the
Years go by?*

If you are a little bit on the eccentric side when you're young, there is a grave risk that you will become exceedingly eccentric in old age. ("Extremely eccentric" in this context is a polite way of saying what most people would call "as mad as a hatter".) Robert's casual interest in collecting soap boxes as a young man gathers pace, and by the time he's fifty it has reached unimaginable proportions. The walls of Robert's home are covered entirely in soap boxes, the furniture is made of soap boxes glued together, and he can talk of nothing else. His friends, who don't share Robert's burning interest in containers for bars of soap, start avoiding him.

"You must come round to my place on Saturday and look at my new soap boxes."

"On Saturday? No, I can't come then I'm afraid. My brother will be crumpling some raisins and I've promised to help him."

Sometimes a different kind of change takes place as you grow older. Instead of certain characteristics becoming more pronounced, they are replaced by their opposites. Little Neil is a real handful when he's a child, he simply can't keep still. As a teenager he drives everybody mad with all his energy and hyperactivity. But when he grows up something strange happens. It's not just that he calms down, but he becomes so calm and passive that he seems to be in a coma. People think he's always on the brink of unconsciousness, and when you are together with him you never know if he's all right or if he's fallen asleep. Somehow or other Neil must have used up all his energy in his youth, and now he's constantly on the back burner and seems to

43

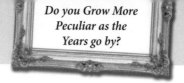

be perfectly happy with that. He moves at a snail's pace and speaks slowly, and nobody who meets him can believe that he was unusually lively as a child. Perhaps it's just as well that Neil has turned out as he has done. If he hadn't been so sluggish and phlegmatic, he would never have been able to carve out for himself such a successful career with a large nationalised company.

Just as Neil changes from hyperactivity to total lethargy, people who are quiet and shy in their young days can change character completely. Shy little Linda, who never dares to say a word but prefers to stand quietly in a corner staring at the floor when she is twenty, has become an unstoppable chatterbox by the time she is forty. It is almost impossible to believe that she is the same person. It's difficult to say what has happened, but Linda's husband Gerald, who first got to know her as a teenager, would like to have the old Linda back. When they first got together she rarely said anything more than yes or no (more often no than yes). Now Linda can speak fifty per cent faster than anybody can listen to her, and the only chance of taking a photograph of her with her mouth closed is to use a slow motion camera. "She's completely hopeless," moans poor Gerald. "She can even get the last word in with an echo."

Do you Grow More Peculiar as the Years go by?

So we can become more peculiar as the years go by, either because our earlier traits of character become so exaggerated that they are almost grotesque; or because we become the opposite of what we were like as children. The taciturn acquire verbal diarrhoea, the shy become pushy and the lively become apathetic. Someone who was a little eccentric when young can become a bit bonkers when old, and someone who tended to be a little pessimistic can become extremely pessimistic. And parsimonious Bruce beats all the records. "Have you heard that Bruce is so mean that when his ancient mum comes to visit him, he hides her false teeth away so that she can't go snacking in between meals?"

Clothes

Clothes

Do we wear different clothes at different stages of our life? Yes, of course we do. Our clothes change as we grow older – not simply because fashion is always changing, but because our taste in clothes changes as the years go by. It's true that the difference in the clothes we wear at various ages is not as great now as is was a few generations ago, but there are still differences.

Do certain clothes signal a certain age? Not always, but quite often. Can you guess the age of a person by looking at the contents of his or her wardrobe? A wardrobe contains eight T-shirts, four pairs of jeans, six pairs of trainers and an empty beer can – is the owner sixty years of age? Another wardrobe contains three double-breasted pinstriped suits, a general's uniform and, right at the back, a full-length red silk dress with tassels: how old is the owner? And what does he do in his spare time?

Younger people are generally more fashion conscious, more "slaves of fashion". They *must* have certain clothes, and in no circumstances can they wear the *wrong* things – to do so would risk being made a laughing stock. If a certain type of jacket or trousers is *in*, it's simply not on to appear in last year's or the year before last's model. There are some middle-aged people (and a few even older ones) who adhere to strict fashion conventions, but to do so is much more common among younger people. Young people don't feel the cold as much as older people do, and hence can wear thinner and lighter items than older people can. (That is presumably why you rarely see a seventy-year-old lady in a miniskirt).

We also wear different shoes at different ages. Young people can wear (and often do) narrow, pointed shoes. Some older people find it difficult to wear shoes like that because of corns, hammer-toe, bunions and various other deformities of the foot. These difficulties and deformities have been caused by wearing narrow, pointed shoes at a younger age. (Which ought to mean that if you refrain from wearing pointed shoes when you are young, you can wear them when you are a little older). It can also be difficult for older women to wear excessively high-heeled shoes (unless they are prepared to risk fracture of the hip joint every week). When you are a little older it is usual to prefer sufficiently wide-fitting, solid-looking shoes that are easy to put on and don't make you look like Cinderella's ugly sisters when they try to force their large feet into Cinderella's glass slippers. Young people can only ever think about wearing wide-fitting shoes (which look as if they were made for Donald Duck) if that is what fashion dictates. If the fashion oracle has prescribed wide-fitting and incredibly ugly footwear, then it is in order for young people to buy such things: otherwise not.

If you are no longer extremely young, how youthfully can you dress before you not only look pathetic, but lay yourself open to the charge of disorderly conduct? Can a fifty-year-old (who isn't a superannuated rock star) wear lilac-coloured snakeskin trousers and an orange T-shirt without seeming desperate? Does it look odd if somebody in late middle age wears tights? Can a pensioner wear hip-hop trousers without looking ridiculous? (Can anybody, irrespective of age, wear hip-hop trousers without looking ridiculous?) Can ancient Grandma wear a thong?

(Ancient Granddad is all in favour.)

In the old days only young people wore jeans. Nowadays you often see eighty-year-olds wearing jeans, and don't think they look odd. In fact, when you are really old you can wear clothes that are as out-dated as you like – nobody expects eighty-year-olds to look as if they have just stepped out of the pages of the latest fashion catalogue. It's perfectly okay to wear a tie eight inches wide or an old-fashioned Borsalino hat with an upturned brim when you are eighty-three. One of the advantages of being very old is that you can wear whatever you like (with the possible exception of wearing trousers back to front). But when you are forty or fifty you are expected to dress appropriately for your age – in other words, not too laughably youthful, nor too absurdly old-fashioned.

Clothes

In fact there is only quite a short period in your life when you can choose your clothes yourself, without interference from your nearest and dearest. As a teenager, your parents interfere with your choice of clothes.

"You can't go out in those trousers! For God's sake, there are big holes in them! And surely you're not contemplating being seen in public wearing that jacket?!"

A little later on in life it's our partners who have views about what we look like. "Surely you're not thinking of wearing that tie with that jacket?! Are you out of your mind? And those trousers! Are you colour-blind? When did you last brush your shoes?"

And eventually it's time for our children to protest about what we are thinking of wearing. "For God's sake, Mum, you can't go out looking like that! I can't allow you to look as if somebody has thrown your clothes onto you with a pitchfork! You look a right mess!"

And as if it weren't enough having to cope with what our children say, our grandchildren also have views about our clothes when we grow even older. "But Granddad, you can't go out looking like that! Do you have to wear red leather trousers and a string vest? Can't you look like other children's granddads?"

Time Passes
More Quickly
the Older
You Get

Time passes more quickly the older you get. You are in a state of constant acceleration as you travel along the axis of time. This is a fact that Einstein missed. As the years pass, they grow shorter and shorter. The process starts after your thirtieth birthday. Between twenty and thirty is exactly ten years. From your thirtieth birthday to the day when you celebrate your fortieth is eight-and-a-half years. Having reached forty, you have exactly seven years before you get to fifty. And it continues in similar fashion. (From your eightieth to your ninetieth birthday is three years and two months.)

When you are young time flows like a slow-moving stream. A leisurely stream in no kind of hurry. When you are a bit older the little stream has become a babbling brook bubbling cheerfully along through the landscape of time. Then time becomes a rushing river. It's about now you start thinking "it's amazing how fast time passes" and "is it Christmas again already?" In the end, time becomes a raging torrent, racing along with colossal force and at such a high speed that it's impossible to resist it. You are hurled forward far too fast in a state of helplessness and you keep having to swallow gallons of unpleasant-tasting cold water, recurrent reminders of how time is running out, dammit. And towards the end it's like falling down a sheer waterfall.

The almost static stream of time we experience in childhood flows faster and faster as time goes by, and even if we manage to avoid the treacherous undercurrents that frequently tempt us, we have no defences when we realise as we grow older that the torrent of time is racing along at a terrifying speed. A good example of the difference in the passage of time for a child and for an adult is the speed at which it moves on Christmas Day. The presents left by Father Christmas in the stockings hanging from the end of the children's beds have been opened and enjoyed, but Daddy says the presents under the tree can't be opened until just before Christmas dinner. There's an hour to go until then. An hour. That is nominally sixty minutes, three thousand six hundred seconds. For Mummy and Daddy that hour means roughly sixty minutes. For the children, the hour is over three hundred minutes, and for Grandma and Granddad that same hour is thirty minutes. For ancient Greatgranddad (ninety-four), whose false teeth are clicking away in anticipation of the Christmas pudding and rum sauce, the hour is less than ten minutes, "and it'll soon be Easter".

It's not only at Christmas that it is obvious how time passes at different speeds for different ages. The summer holiday is endless for a small child. For the child's parents the holiday is over almost before it has begun. The holiday comes around at last: now they can both rest and be active, do things there had been no time to do earlier, and enjoy simply lazing around. But suddenly it's all over. Two rainy weeks in the summer cottage with their unpleasant cousins, a few weeks that simply vanished, and a week of quarrelling about why they should, or

shouldn't, rent a sailing boat. Wherever did that holiday get to? Now it's autumn, winds, darkness and colds. November comes sneaking up, the stress of Christmas is lurking round the corner, and "It'll soon be Easter," says Greatgranddad (ninety-four).

So much more happens when you are young than when you are older. Impressions are more numerous, more novel and deeper. You are always experiencing something new, which makes time pass more slowly. When you are older one day is much the same as the next, experiences and impressions are not as novel nor as powerful, and time has accelerated. A lot happens when you are between twenty and thirty, or between thirty and forty. You get married, have children (not necessarily in that order), make a career, get divorced, lose your driving licence, re-marry, get the sack, have your teeth whitened, and start to wonder what you are going to do with your life and if you should repaint the hall. Perhaps in mint-green.

When you are eighty-four, not nearly as much happens, generally speaking. You get up in the morning (ouch, pains in your joints), have a bite to eat, think about your stomach, go for a short walk (ouch), watch the occasional TV programme, forget to take your medicine, think about your stomach and drink a cup of wishy-washy coffee and eat a sugar-free bun that tastes like chipboard. A whole day lasts for

three hours and twenty minutes. (If you give the coffee and chipboard bun a miss, the day lasts for two hours and forty-five minutes. It's "a bloody short day", as the parrot said when there was a power cut at breakfast time and the lights went out.)

Can you get time to pass more slowly when you grow a little older? Do we have to see sixty-minute hours shrink to forty-five minutes, thirty minutes, twenty minutes? You can try to make time pass a little more slowly by packing your days and your life with events and experiences. This doesn't mean that late middle-aged people have to re-marry, start competing in Formula One races and open a chain of country-wide dry-cleaning shops or massage parlours. (Although doing that is not a bad idea if you want to be active and acquire new experiences.) There are other things you can fill your life with in order to feel that you really are alive, and so avoid the acceleration effect of time that goes hand-in-hand with a monotonous everyday lifestyle. It doesn't matter so much what you do, as long as you like doing it and it doesn't come under the heading of disorderly behaviour in a public place. By filling your life with new experiences and impressions, you can try to turn thirty-minute hours into forty-minute ones, if not more.

Hair

What happens to our hair when we grow older? As we wave goodbye to the past, do we have to say farewell to our hair? That is sometimes the case, but it's not the only thing that happens. A lot of people's hair has a tendency to change colour as time passes. With men it tends to turn grey, and with women it can become either grey or blond. For some reason (sometimes, at least) women can dye their hair without it being seen that it's dyed. It's more of a problem with men. When men dye their hair it becomes either lifeless and unnaturally crow-black, or ridiculously reddish. The reddishness surrounds the hair like a sort of aura when it is doing its best to look brown or blond. In both cases, both the strangely black and the amusingly red, the owner might just as well wear a sign on his head saying: "Look at me, I've dyed my hair!"

A divorced woman, who was looking out for a new possible husband, used to say that it was good that some men dyed their hair, "because then you can see immediately which ones have no self-confidence."

But it's not only the colour of your hair that can change: the amount of hair you have is usually affected by the ageing process. (This applies more to men than to women, of course.) Their hairline creeps upwards and their hair thins out. Men who are affected in this way early in life (it can happen in your twenties, and is usually hereditary) generally claim that it is due to the fact that they have unusually large amounts of testosterone. To what extent this claim influences the women of their acquaintance is difficult to say. An old saying suggests that: "The less hair you have to comb, the more face you have to wash." In the end you can have a face that stretches as far as

the back of your head. That is probably what is meant by the familiar expression that so-and-so "is long in the face."

As some men don't like to be thin-haired, they do whatever they can to conceal the fact. This can result in some very strange hairstyles that are both touching and pathetic. Some men allow their hair to grow very long at the back of their heads, and then comb it forward over the bald pate. It usually looks very funny. You can also allow the hair on one side of your head to grow long, then comb it sideways over the bald patch. This looks quite funny, but not quite as funny as the forward-combing variation. In both cases you must be careful not to expose your hair to the wind. And so, if you have one of these interesting hairstyles, you should avoid going out of doors when it's windy; nor should you enter premises where there are fans or powerful air conditioning. A blast of air can make the most stylish gentleman look ridiculous.

Some men compensate for the bald or thinly covered crown of the head by growing their hair long at the back. Not in order to comb it forward over the bald patch, but to demonstrate that they certainly do have some long, thick hair somewhere. It's as if they want to say: "I might not have so much hair on the top of my head, but look how much I have at the back!" And they are right, of course.

It is possible to transplant hair, but that is often both costly and difficult. A simpler way of concealing your thinning hair is to acquire a toupee. A good toupee can make you look at least fifteen years sillier. You must also ensure that the toupee is fixed firmly in place, both when it's windy and when you are leaning over your bowl of soup.

In recent years it has become fashionable for men to attempt to conceal their incipient baldness by shaving the whole of their heads. Doing that makes them look completely bald. It's a little difficult to understand the thinking behind this. Does removing all the hair on your head make you look less bald? Is that the way they are thinking? Do they hope people will look at their shaved heads and think: "He's actually got a thick mane of hair, but as he's a bit mad he's shaved it all off."? Would you prefer to be regarded as a bit mad rather than a bit on the bald side? Why? It's not shameful to be bald.

The easiest way of hiding the fact that you are grey-haired or bald (and hence not so young any more) is to wear a cap. A young man's cap in a bright colour makes you younger at a stroke. Or at least makes you look like an elderly gentleman with a brightly coloured young man's cap.

A special variant when it comes to hair and age is facial hair. (To make things easier, we're only talking about men now.) If you have a beard or a moustache, does it make you look older or younger? When you are young, you generally look older if you grow a beard. Beards make you think of elderly people (Father Christmas, God, George Bernhard Shaw). But if you grow a beard when you are fifty years old, for instance, does that make you look younger because it's mainly young men who have beards? And if you have a beard, do you look younger if you shave it off? Or does it make you look older? Do you look on the old side if you have a beard on only half of your face? Would anybody bother to worry about how old you are if you only have half a beard? Isn't it more likely that people would ask themselves: Why does he only have a beard on the right-hand side of his face? For Christ's sake, he can't be all there.

And they would probably be right.

Health

*When do you start becoming interested in your health? Generally
speaking, your health is not something you think about when you are
young. Young people don't usually worry about occasional symptoms,
unless they are hypochondriacs. You can be a hypochondriac at any
age, and for a genuine hypochondriac every ailment or symptom is a
sign of some life-threatening illness or other. Age plays no part at all,
which means that a twenty-one-year-old who has a slight pain in the
chest is convinced that it is the first stage of a heart attack. A twenty-
three-year-old with sufficiently strong hypochondriac tendencies who
forgets something can be convinced that his forgetfulness is due to
widespread arteriosclerosis and acute, galloping senile decay. Nothing
is impossible for an enthusiastic hypochondriac. No matter how old or
young you are, you can be quite sure the reason you are feeling cold
is malaria.*

"Malaria can make you shiver with cold!"

*"Come on, it's minus eighteen degrees and you're only wearing a thin
jacket! That's why you feel cold!"*

"You think so? You don't think it's malaria?"

If you are not a hypochondriac, you don't usually think about how
well you are when you are young. As you grow older, it's not unusual
to start suffering from various ailments and pains, and you get to
an age when you wake up every morning and amuse yourself by
counting up how many pains you have. As you lie in bed you can
shout out the number of pains to your partner – or if you don't have
one, to yourself. "Four! That's not so bad. Mind you, I haven't counted

my heartburn – I don't usually get that until after I've drunk my coffee." Or: "Eight! A new personal record! I don't think I'll bother to get up today."

If you are unlucky, when you get older you can suffer from a number of ailments that more or less spoil your daily life. But people react differently to the same symptoms at different ages. When you get stomach ache at the age of thirty or so, you think it is probably due to yesterday's Italian-Mexican-inspired dinner consisting of anchovy pizza, baked beans, marinated chicken wings in pepper sauce, guacamole with tabasco, French fried potatoes, beer, soft whey-cheese and apple pie. (The last-mentioned component was just to ensure there was something English there as well). The thirty-year-old doesn't think it's strange that he has stomach ache after all that. But a forty-year-old doesn't think about yesterday's dinner, he suspects a stomach ulcer or perhaps a gallstone. He knows a lot of people with stomach problems who take popular remedies to counter them. Perhaps he ought to start taking some such medicine as well – it's almost anti-social not to do so. No doubt it's best to to contact his GP.

A sixty-year-old with stomach pains knows it can be something dangerous. He knows lots of people with stomach problems. Both your stomach and your large intestine can start playing up, and

somebody at work also developed liver problems. But he was a heavy drinker, according to Ellen in accounts. If you have a copy of the *Reader's Digest Health Guide* you will know that stomach ache can be caused by dissecting stomach aortic aneurysm. It's not all that common, but still. So there are big differences in the diagnosis you plump for according to how old you are. A thirty-year-old who coughs thinks he has a bit of a cold, whereas a sixty-year-old reacts quite differently, especially if he smokes. A twenty-five-year-old with a pain in the leg thinks it was due to last week's work-out in the gym, while a fifty-year-old thinks his joints are worn out and an eighty-year-old suspects poor blood circulation: "I think the doctor said my blood-vessels were so calcified that they are harder than my muscles."

When women reach the menopause they can get all kinds of symptoms they never had when they were thirty-five. It's not just sweating, hot flushes and mood changes: other symptoms can make themselves felt. There have been discussions about whether or not men have a similar change of life: some maintain they do, others say there are no physiological grounds to support the claim, and that if it does exist, it's a psychological phenomenon. Whether or not there is in fact a male menopause, it can safely be said that when many men reach a certain age they have prostate troubles, a reminder that time's ever-rolling stream eventually dries up.

People who smoke have found a good way of both growing old more quickly, and at the same time increasing the probability of not growing very old. The classic exchange sums it up nicely:

"We smokers are also human, you know!"

"Yes, but not for as long as the rest of us."

Even if you are a non-smoker it's not unusual for some ailment or other to afflict you eventually. The older you become, the greater the risk of more or less serious health problems cropping up. If you are lucky enough (?) to grow really old, the odds are that you will not escape ailments and illnesses altogether. The ageing process naturally means that parts of your body are likely to function less than perfectly. What was it the old man said? – "I've got pains everywhere, and what doesn't hurt doesn't work."

As you grow older and various ailments kick in, you may need to take medication. Sometimes various medicines are necessary. You have to keep abreast of which medicines to take, why you need to take them, and how and when to take them. Every new visit to the doctor's often means new medicines being prescribed, and in the end you have more jars, bottles and tubes than any normal person can keep up with. What follows is a patient's inner monologue about his medication. It is very close to the truth.

"What exactly was it the doctor said about my medication? At first I thought he said I shouldn't take any medicines, but then he said that it was important I should take the medicines in accordance with the instructions. I think he said I should take them three times a day, once every morning and every evening. Can that be right? It sounds a bit odd. I mean, I have several different kinds of medicine. What are these little red tablets for? They were for my stomach, I think – no, it was the white ones that are for my stomach, so these must be for my blood pressure. The doctor said my blood pressure was too low. Or did he say that it was too high? There was something wrong with my blood pressure anyway. And these little brown pills, when am I supposed to take them? Was it just before or just after I'd gone to sleep? These capsules are for my knees, I think. I've never taken them, they look so big, it can't be easy to swallow them. Three times a day: that sounds a bit much, surely one a day will be enough. At most. I haven't a clue where these oblong tablets come from. What on earth can they be good for? Were those the ones for my blood sugar? Or are they the ones in that little jar over there? They can't be much good for anything at all, they're far too small.

My God, what a lot of medication I've got. I'll have to buy a bigger medicine cabinet to hold them all. The old cupboard is overfull. A lot of the stuff needs to be thrown away. Where does this jar come from? I don't recognize it. I wonder what those pills are for. I'd better take some of them, they look rather nice. A pretty yellow colour. I think I'll throw these green ones away – wasn't it those that somebody at the pharmacy said had all kinds of side effects? Where they for my chest? Or were they for heartburn? I think those were the ones there was an article about in the paper. They can give you hallucinations. Or did they make you feel sick and give you a headache? Something like that.

I think they are the tablets that Eric's brother-in-law used to take. He died. Something to do with his lymph nodes. Or his heart. I wonder if I dare tell the doctor these tablets aren't doing me any good – not that I know what they are for..."

Generally speaking, you'll need to visit the doctor more often as you grow older. Blood pressure has to be checked, your heart listened to, your stomach needs to be squeezed and blood samples taken. Round about the age of forty, most people start to wonder if they ought to have a health check. Nobody has any such thought when they are thirty, but it's probably high time now. You hear so much about all the things that have happened to people, so it's best to undergo a general medical examination. You feel in good form – but better safe than sorry. Have a few tests and get the doctor to check your heart and lungs, and ask whether it's normal to lose as much hair as you've lost lately.

Health checks are no doubt a good thing in certain circumstances, but you ought to be aware that testing is not an exact science. If you undergo enough tests, there is always a risk that one will suggest something is wrong with you, even though you are perfectly healthy. A rogue test often results in more tests, which lead to more tests, and you frequently end up having even more tests. Nevertheless, it is a

good idea to check your state of health now and again, and if you are lucky, you might hear some encouraging words from your doctor:

"Mr Wilson, your heart is going to last you all your life!" (What on earth does that mean?)

Or: "Mrs Chapman, you have the body of a forty-year-old!"

"But I am forty?"

"There you are, you see: what did I tell you?"

Unfortunately, the older you grow, the more you learn about the mystifying labyrinth that is the National Health Service. But that doesn't have to be the case, of course. If you are lucky you can live to be ninety without ever having had the doubtful pleasure of waltzing around the corridors of the NHS. But for most people, the passage of time means a closer acquaintance with blood pressure cuffs, stethoscopes, blood tests and medicine bottles. You know that you are no longer young when your little black telephone book is full of the numbers of doctors, nurses and physiotherapists. Moreover, your medicine cabinet is fuller with a wider range of products than your bar cupboard.

Topics of
Conversation

What we talk about with our friends changes as the years go by. Needless to say, there are some topics we discuss for as long as we live (the weather, taxes, Donald Duck's Christmas celebrations) and which crop up irrespective of how old we are; but some topics are age-specific. In our twenties we talk a lot about the opposite sex, hobbies, and whether anybody can lend us a couple of hundred pounds until next Thursday. We discuss our love-life problems, or boast about our amazing successes with the opposite sex (or with the same sex, as the case may be). But gradually, as we float along with the tide of life, we start to discuss gruel, napkins and breast-feeding. We argue about the advantages and disadvantages of various types of children's clothes, and become specialists in PVC-coated trousers and all-weather bootees, Continental size 23. We exchange information with our friends about ear-ache and chickenpox, and the alcohol-inspired yarns we used to spin about fantastic Saturday nights seem to belong to the far distant past – although it's not all that many years since we were there.

Not long after the discussions about the merits of children's trousers and fevers, it is often time to start talking about your work. How much there is to do, how stressed you are, and what an out-and-out lunatic your boss is. "For Christ's sake, he's an absolute idiot! I don't understand how they could possibly have put him in charge. He's now going on about how we must cut down on staff in our department. The only thing we need to cut down is him! With a machete!"

Your job and your prospective career can be a favourite topic of conversation for a number of years. Work takes up a large part of our

time and our thoughts, and we naturally feel obliged to talk about what lies closest to our hearts. Whether other people want to hear about it or not.

"Can you believe it, at work yesterday they were going to begin cleaning up the lift shafts, and they were going to start on our floor: and I told them it made more sense to start at the bottom and work their way up."

"You don't say? Have you seen any interesting films lately?"

"Then that idiot said that they always started at the top and worked their way down. They were intending to oil the bearer cable with No. 8 grease, and I told them that for heaven's sake, they ought to use No. 5 grease on the bearer cable, but that idiot said they'd always used No. 8. Have you ever heard anything so stupid in all your life?"

"Hmm, yes, well... Did you see the match on the telly yesterday? Liverpool were terrific, don't you think?"

"Then they decided that the transmitter accumulator needed to be changed!"

"Anyway, I have to go now – it was great talking to you!"

"Hang on, don't go yet! I haven't told you what they did with the control cable in the lift shaft..."

Time passes, and suddenly we find ourselves sitting with our friends, discussing divorces. We start talking about John-Paul and Monica – who would have thought that they would get divorced? And it's such a pity about the children. After a while we talk about Marianne and George who are about to split up – that's not much of a surprise in

fact, but it's such a pity about the children. And before we know where we are we are spelling out details of our own impending divorce. It's both expected and unexpected, and needless to say it's all the fault of our partner and it's such a pity about the children, but we simply can't go on like this. Our partner is impossible to live with, especially after the partner discovered that we'd been having an affair on the side for the past couple of years. "No, we just can't go on like this, shouting and quarrelling from morning till night. We should never have got married, it was bound to turn out like this. It's as I've always said: the main cause of divorce is marriage."

There's no end to what can be said about divorces, and they can be discussed until the cows come home. How can the urgent problem of finding somewhere to live be solved?

"Can I stay with you for a few nights? Just until I find a place of my own?"

"Er, I don't really know. Our place is rather cramped..."

"Only a few nights, a week at most. I can sleep on the sofa, I promise I won't be any trouble. Just a few nights."

"Well... all right... if it's only going to be a few nights I suppose we can manage."

"Excellent! Many thanks. A week at most. Maybe two."

Six months later the divorcee is still sleeping on the sofa: "It's not so easy to find a flat, you know, but I think the problem will be solved next week. A bloke at work knows somebody who is going to sub-let his bed-sit. What's for dinner tonight?"

A divorce always produces new topics of conversation with your friends. Who is going to take what, how are the finances going to be solved, how will it be possible to pay the lawyers, and who's going to have custody of the dog? "It's the finest labrador in the whole world. I'm certainly going to keep that dog! There's no way I'm going to give way on that score. And we still have to agree about the children, about who's going to have them."

The children are now teenagers, with all the problems that state involves. Divorce doesn't exactly make the problems any easier. And we now get the feeling that we're not exactly young any more. How did this come about? Not long ago we were young, happy and without a care in the world. Now we are no longer young, nor happy, but we are certainly careworn. And we have a new topic of conversation.

"He's out gallivanting all night long, I don't know what to do. God only knows what he gets up to during the night – I worry that he might end up in some peculiar gang or other. He takes no notice of whatever I say to him. How do you know if your kids are on drugs? Is it something you can see in their eyes?"

"Yes, I think so. Their pupils become enormous. Or do they become tiny? I can't remember. I have similar problems with Lily. She's always out, and when I ask her where she's been, she doesn't answer. Last Saturday she came home on Sunday. I don't know what to do with her. And she's started smoking as well."

"Thank your lucky stars that it's just ordinary cigarettes."

Divorces, problematic teenagers and an increasing awareness that we are not getting any younger can start us off drinking a bit more than we used to do. This is not something we talk about – on the contrary, we refuse to acknowledge it even to ourselves and are equipped with a bucketful of explanations and excuses.

"I've had such a stressful day today, I really do need a little drink. A little drink won't do you any harm. Or two. They're only little ones, and not all that strong. Just ordinary vodka. Three little drinks aren't dangerous, considering the stress I've had to put up with. The divorce has been very hard work, and next week it's my turn to have the children. Johnny's hopeless nowadays – he takes no notice of what you tell him, and is out on the town all night long. I hope he hasn't started drinking. I could do with another little drink – I've only had two. Or three. Just one more. Or two. I need that. Life isn't so easy. And I'm not as young as I used to be. I'm starting to get big bags under my eyes: I don't understand where they come from. I think I'd better have another drink. Just a little one."

Children grow older (they're not the only ones), and we acquire new topics of conversation when our offspring get married and we are presented with sons-in-law and daughters-in-law. Obviously these incomers must be embraced, whether we like them or not.

"To tell you the truth, I can't understand what Nicholas sees in Annie. I'd hoped for a better daughter-in-law than Annie. But Nicholas seems to like her. I don't want to sound negative, but she really is – what shall I say? – annoying. She really is. And stupid. And

badly brought up, and lazy. She is – and I say this with the best will in the world – an unpleasant slut. Nicholas deserves somebody much better. I do my best to accept her as a member of the family, but it's not easy. A stupid, unpleasant slut – that's certainly not what we'd hoped to have as a daughter-in-law, by Jove no. I don't want to sound negative, but she really is the pits."

Time rolls on inexorably and the next big topic of conversation is grandchildren. People who acquire grandchildren are generally obsessed by them, and unwilling to talk about anything else. With a bit of free association it's always possible to find an excuse to talk about your grandchildren, no matter what the other person is talking about.

"Did you see that the minimum lending rate is going to be raised? I wonder how that will affect the policy rate. What do you think?"

"The minimum lending rate? Yes, I saw that on the telly – little Teddy thinks it's such good fun, watching the telly. We often watch *Peter Pan* on video and Teddy usually imitates Peter Pan, and once when we were at a funfair Teddy said..."

Sometimes the associations need to be a little more volatile, but with a little goodwill it works out all right.

"What do you think about the domestic political situation in Indonesia? Things seem a bit turbulent there."

"Yes, and not only there. Little Teddy had a stomach upset last week, but he's a lot better now. We were in the park yesterday, playing on the swings, and you'd never believe what he got up to. Hang on a minute and I'll tell you..."

If you speak enthusiastically about your grandchildren to somebody who doesn't have any, that person won't understand what you are talking about. It's like trying to describe a magnificent giant firework display to somebody who wasn't there. "And then, can you imagine, the whole sky was lit up by enormous constellations of stars in green and yellow and red, and then they changed shape and became sort of round and oblong, and changed colour at the same time, and spread out like a fan. It was the most fantastic sight I've seen in all my life!"

"You don't say, really? Good heavens, is that the time? I must be on my way now."

On the other hand, if you talk about your grandchildren to somebody who also has some, they understand why you sound like you do, but needless to say they want to talk about their own grandchildren instead. It can become an exciting duel with burnished grandchildren as weapons. As in all wars, the first casualty is the truth.

"You should see little Teddy, he's only one, but he can build incredibly high houses of wooden bricks all by himself. He balances loads of bricks on top of one another."

"Really? Little Sally already draws lovely pictures although she's only one-and-a-half. She's very precocious."

"Draws? Little Teddy paints marvellous little pictures, often seascapes."

"Did I say draw? Sally paints in oils, splendid portraits: she's painted all the family. Beautifully controlled brush strokes, a bit like the masters of the late Renaissance."

"Teddy doesn't only paint, of course. He's writing a book. It's a novel of ideas with historical themes."

"Sally has just finished a popular science book about the fundamentals of philosophy. She wrote it in less than a week. Using crayons."

"Little Teddy has been offered a post as guest Professor in Harvard. As soon as he's learnt to talk."

"Isn't it marvellous to have grandchildren?"

"It certainly is!"

It's not only grandchildren who illustrate the passage of time, your own parents do that as well. As you are growing older, your parents are growing even older. The increasingly elderly parents are another topic of conversation connected with age.

"I don't know what I'm going to do with my old mum. She's started to be gaga, and I'd better not get started on her memory!"

"I know, I know – I have the same problem with my dad. He has eleven different items of medication to see to, and he has no idea about how or why he should take them. He rings me three times a day and asks how he is."

"My mum rings me in the middle of the night to tell me she's having difficulty in going to sleep."

"I don't know what I'm going to do with my old dad. What do you do with old codgers when they can't look after themselves any more? He has a home help who he hates and he refuses to let her in."

"There' a lot to be said for the old custom of ancient dodderers jumping over the edge of a precipice. But you can't say that nowadays, of course. But what can you do? Last week I was with my mum at A & E. We had to wait for four hours and when the doctor finally turned up, my mum had forgotten why she was there.

"What did you do?"

"I drove her home. What else could we do? I suggested to the doctor that they should keep her in until she remembered what was wrong with her, but that wasn't possible."

"It's difficult to get into hospital."

"Yes, especially when those big swing doors keep getting stuck."

Your ancient parents (that you don't know what to do with) are not the only ones who suffer from illnesses, ailments and health problems. We ourselves are affected quite often as we grow older. (See also the chapter *Health*.) All kinds of ailments become favourite topics of conversation, and we exchange symptoms and medical experiences with our friends.

"How did your liver tests turn out?"

"Not too bad, thank you; the results are a bit better, but my blood pressure has gone up. How's your stomach?"

"Quite good. I'm trying a new softening laxative that seems to be working pretty well."

"Really? That sounds interesting. What's it called?"

So we can reach a point where softening laxatives are an interesting topic of conversation. When we grow even older we start discussing not only our own ailments and symptoms, but other people's illnesses as well.

"I heard that Johnson has had a stroke."

"Good grief! Who's Johnson?"

"I don't know, but it's awful even so."

Since we have all kinds of physical problems when we are a bit older, it's as well to have recourse to a little collection of medical practitioners who can help us out when needed. And so we discuss not only our symptoms and medicines with our friends, but we discuss our doctors as well.

"Dr Steinfinkel is really good. He's a bit scatterbrained at times and mixes up his patients and so on, but he's really good. And very pleasant as well – I know lots of people who go to see him even when they are healthy."

"Why do they go to him when they are healthy?"

"Because he's so nice. And besides, he's so good that he always finds something wrong with you. No matter how healthy you are, he always finds something wrong with you. He's really good."

"Hmm, he sounds very good. I go to Dr Johnson – he's very good as well. And he's quite famous. There was quite a lot about him in the press a few years ago."

"Really? What did they say?"

"I don't remember exactly, it was something to do with the Social Services and his authorisation, I'm not sure of the details. They printed a big picture of him."

"That sounds great. If he's been in the papers he must be good."

A topic of conversation that crops up no matter how old you are, but which increases in frequency and intensity as you grow older, is your

memory. Thirty-year-olds remember what it was like to be twenty, forty-year-olds remember what it was like to be thirty, and fifty-year-olds remember what it was like to be eighteen. The older you become, the more memories you have to talk about. (This continues until you get to a certain point when you are so old that your memories begin to grow less rather than more.) When you are sufficiently old, and have lots of memories but haven't yet started to forget them, you might well talk a lot and at great length about "the old days". Nearly every sentence begins with "When I was a lad..." or "I remember when..." If you haven't lived an unusually exciting and eventful life, there is a distinct risk that you will soon bore everybody stiff with your "When I was a lad..." or "I remember when...", followed by a sleep-inducing monologue. Non-events come tumbling out one after another in a never-ending stream. The only chance of putting a stop to this flood of uninteresting memories is to interrupt and change the subject. Talking about your own ailments is always an attractive option.

"I recall another occasion when I was going to buy a pair of socks and..."

"Absolutely fascinating! Speaking of socks, I've been having quite a lot of pain in my foot for some time now, around my ankle, sort of, and above it. I had pains in my foot last year as well, but where it hurt was further forward then – that was about the same time as I was having trouble with my stomach, and not only my stomach in fact, but..."

And it goes on like that until we're so old that we can no longer remember what we've forgotten that we ought to remember.

Do you Become **Cleverer when** You Get Older?

Do you become cleverer when you get older?

One need have no hesitation in giving a very definite answer to that question: Hmm, perhaps.

But surely you ought to become cleverer as the years go by? More experience, more worldly wisdom – that would certainly seem to suggest that you become cleverer. But then again, have you noticed how many elderly politicians there are? Do they seem to be intellectual giants?

But don't you become more mature as you grow older? Increased maturity brings with it more considered thinking which in turn entails greater sagacity. One would think so, but the question is: does that apply to everybody? If you are decidedly unclever (that sounds better than "as thick as three sawn planks") when you are young, it's by no means certain that you will be cleverer when you are old. Naturally, you learn things as you journey through life: but learning and knowledge are not the same as wisdom.

As you grow older, you generally acquire a greater understanding of yourself. You realise, often reluctantly, that you have a number of less attractive sides to your character that you hadn't noticed before. ("What? Are you saying I'm mean? That's the silliest thing I've ever heard! And stop looking out of the window so often – it wears out

the glass.") You become aware that you are not perfect, and that your previous mantra "It's not easy to be humble when you're as outstanding as I am" doesn't really ring true. Having acquired insight into your real self, you can then start looking at the world in a different light: and that also gives you something to ponder on. What do the new views look like? What do you have ahead of you? What do you have behind you? Can you perhaps make use of what you see in the rear view mirror to affect the view in front of you? Can your new insights affect your prospects? Yes, if you have become a little wiser, they can.

Do people become more sure about things when they grow older? More sure about what? That it is most often silly to be too sure about anything? In that case shouldn't one become less sure about things, the older and wiser one grows? (Always assuming people ever become wiser as they grow older).

"It's only stupid people who are positive about anything!"

"Are you sure about that?"

"Absolutely positive!"

Young people often think they know everything, and have the answers to all questions. They know everything, from the answer to questions about the meaning of life to how you connect your computer to your toaster in order to make Internet-toasted granary bread. But as the years go by, most

people realise that neither the questions nor the answers are as obvious as they thought they were when they were young. This insight must no doubt be classed as increased wisdom. But what about experience? As you grow older your experience of life increases. Is all experience beneficial? Or might it be better to be a little naive at times? If you are unlucky, experience of life can be the harbinger of cynicism. "I think you should always think the best about people, for then you are often disappointed and in the end you are so disillusioned that nothing affects you any more."

Someone once said: "Experience is the comb that life gives us when we've lost all our hair." Is that true? When we have acquired the experience and wisdom that old age presents us with, it's too late to make use of the fact. When we are elderly we have discovered how we ought to have acted when we were younger. Once the race is run, we find out which horses we ought to have backed.

Thank you, thank you very much.

Another illuminating quotation goes: "When you reach the age of seventy-five you have learnt everything. All you need to do is to try to remember it." That is not always so easy.

If we don't become wiser when we grow older, we shall just have to make do with the fact that we are older. And when we are old we can say: "I used to be young and daft, but now I'm quite old and that's not so daft."

Exercise is good for you, no matter how old you are. Does exercise make you older? That's a question it's hard to answer, but it feels like that after a five-mile run. It doesn't matter what kind of exercise you take, the important thing is that you do it. You can walk, jog, cycle, swim, or do all those things at the same time.

Does a run through the woods make you younger? Or does it just make you out of breath? We've all seen those seventy-year-old joggers staggering along the dedicated track, puffing and panting, and looking as if they're going to drop dead at any moment. But is that merely what it looks like? Are they in fact eighty-eight years old, and it's all that jogging that makes them look much younger? Surely they can't be worn-out fifty-year-olds who have aged prematurely because of all that running?

The problem with jogging is that it's so boring. Have you ever seen a jogger laugh? They sweat and pant, pull faces and groan and wonder what the hell they are doing as they gasp desperately for breath. It's all very well prancing around in the woods when you are twenty or thirty years old – but what about when you are fifty or sixty? Not to mention seventy. Your knees hurt, your hips creak, and your heart pounds like a tilthammer. And you think: can this really be good for me? It feels as if your lungs are bursting, and there's a steep gradient just ahead. You

feel you want assurance in writing that this self-torture really is good for you, and preferably also makes you younger.

Of course, you don't have to go out running (especially if it's raining). There are lots of other ways of exercising. You can play tennis or golf, go for walks, practise taekwondo or read a good book. (It's perhaps doubtful if reading a book counts as real exercise, but one shouldn't be fanatical about this.)

What kind of exercise is most suitable at different ages? Some kinds are fine no matter how old you are – going for walks, playing golf and swimming, for instance. On the other hand it's doubtful if old people ought to devote themselves to ice hockey (not at an elite level, at least) or boxing.

Whatever kind of exercise you choose, it's important to have the right clothing. The dictates of fashion apply even to exercise kit, and needless to say, you can't go out jogging in the woods dressed any old how. All joggers, irrespective of age, need special jogging trainers with padded stabilising comfort collars, sure-grip contoured cushioned footbeds, and lightweight flexible uppers. These shoes are a pleasure to sprain your ankle in. If you really want to look youthful, you also need neon-yellow luminescent tights and a silvery-blue headband. A headband is both attractive and practical. It looks good, and it also holds your head together when it feels as if it's about to burst after a couple of miles at much too high a speed.

A classic way of proving both to yourself and to others that you are still young is to take part in the London Marathon. You can enter the London Marathon at any age, but it's more important to run it when you are forty, fifty, sixty or seventy than when you are twenty or thirty. Being a middle-aged man and completing the London Marathon is a rite of passage, a test of manhood that shows you are still both young and virile. (The London Marathon is the equivalent of a little red sports car for this age category, and is much cheaper.) A few days after completing the London Marathon (when the nurses have removed the drip and the oxygen tube) you can boast about your achievement to your friends of the same age. "It was a piece of cake. A bit steep on Constitution Hill, but no problem. It's just a matter of keeping going. I whizzed along like a greyhound, in fact."

Not a word about the heroic efforts of the hospital nurses or the air ambulance crew.

When you are really old you might find going out for a run less than appealing. You might well find it more attractive to satisfy your athletic aspirations by watching sports programmes on the television. Or you could play chess. If playing chess makes you out of breath, you are probably out of condition and ought perhaps to consider taking a little exercise even so.

Finances

"I have enough money to last me the rest of my life – provided I die before Thursday next week."

The above quotation sums up neatly the fact that we need money all our life. Irrespective of our age, we need money: our finances are just as important for a thirty-year-old as for a seventy-year-old. How does our financial situation change as we grow older? It's a very individual matter and hence impossible to answer. We often have too little money during the first half of our life (when we really need it), but if we're lucky we have more money in the second half of our life, when we may well have fewer desires and needs. Not infrequently we don't have enough money for the first half of our lives and not enough money for the second half of our lives either. (How it will be in the life after this one is not so easy to say, but no doubt there will be cash machines there as well.)

How important is it to have money at different stages of your life? Somebody (presumably Oscar Wilde) said: "When you are young you think money is the most important thing in your life; when you are old, you know it is." But it's doubtful whether this is true. When we are young we would like to be extremely rich (preferably without having to exert ourselves too much), and young people often have a rather flippant and irresponsible attitude towards money. If you have a bit of

money, you like to blow it on something enjoyable. If you are young and single you often regard food and rent as unforeseen expenses, whereas such things as clothes and entertainment are given priority in the budget you don't bother to make. "Money doesn't matter," you might well say in the wishful hope that things will turn out all right anyway. If a crisis occurs, there is always somebody you can borrow a bit of money from. In normal circumstances your attitude towards money and financial affairs changes as you grow older. Needless to say, however, there are those who don't fit into the normal range and find themselves at one extreme or other of the abnormal peripheries. There are those who are very thrifty even at an early age, and they become even meaner as they grow older until they are in their seventies, when they have a bulging bank account but don't think they can afford to eat anything other than blood pudding, and only small portions of that. At the other end of the scale is the individual who has a total lack of understanding when it comes to financial matters and the value of money, and continues in the same style for the rest of his life. All money flows out much more quickly than it flows in, and financial crises and catastrophes follow one another in rapid succession. It is quite amusing when people at either end of these two financial extremes get married. It starts as early as the honeymoon.

"Let's go for a trip round the world – first class flights and luxury hotels all the way. What do you say to that?"

"No, no, are you out of your mind?! I thought we might go cycling in Yorkshire and stay in youth hostels. Or we could borrow my brother-in-law's tent. It leaks a bit when it rains, but we can borrow it for free."

"A tent? That leaks? I think we should visit the Maldives, Mauritius, Hong Kong, Paris, Australia..."

"If you don't think a week cycling around Yorkshire would be any good, we could go cycling in Lancashire instead. We can take packed meals. Tins of baked beans in tomato sauce that we can heat up on a spirit stove."

Marriages like this don't normally last very long.

We regard money somewhat differently at different ages. What does a twenty-year-old think when he suddenly finds himself with a hundred pounds to spare? He thinks: "A hundred quid! Terrific! I can go on a pub crawl tonight. Or maybe I'll buy that cool-looking shirt I saw with double sleeves and a hand-sewn stiff collar for £95?"

A thirty-year-old with a hundred pounds to spare thinks: "A hundred pounds? That's good news. The youngster could do with new shoes, and so could I. I wonder if there's enough for both of us?"

When you are forty you put the hundred pounds in your savings account. "Best to put it by for a rainy day. You never know what might happen."

A fifty-year-old thinks: "A hundred pounds. That's excellent. It will help to pay some of my back tax. God only knows how I'm going to get the rest of the money."

A sixty-year-old has already begun to feel the chilly wind of his approaching retirement: "I'll save this money until I'm on my pension – it'll come in useful then, the pension won't be enough to live on."

But what about the thoughts of an eighty-year-old regarding the extra hundred pounds? "A hundred pounds? Terrific! I can go on a

96

pub crawl tonight. Or maybe I'll buy that cool-looking shirt I saw with double sleeves and a hand-sewn stiff collar for £95?"

One's attitude towards saving or splashing out with money varies according to age. When you are young, you may well think there's nothing wrong with being lavish – more money will always turn up. As time goes by you begin to realise that having some savings would be a boon, but when you are really old you might perhaps think it's time to start splashing out again. "Save? For what? For when? I'm eighty-eight years old – why should I save? I've been saving all my life, now it's time to throw money about! By the way, what do you think of my six new shirts with double sleeves and hand-sewn stiff collars?"

It's understandable that people should think it's time to splash out (always assuming you have any money to splash out) when they are old. When you are young there is always something to save up for: a holiday, a new car, a house, an exclusive fountain pen or a piece of turbot for dinner. When you are old, you might well think you have done enough saving. If you are eighty, you don't need to save for your pension any more – you ought to have thought of that a long time ago. On the other hand, it might seem odd to begin thinking about saving for your retirement when you are twenty-five. Retirement seems so far away, and you think you need all the money you can get right now.

Besides, it's not so easy to know where you should keep the money you save. In shares, which might go down in value? In stocks that might collapse? In banks that try to rob you of all your money? Under your mattress?

Your home is an important part of your life, and something that often has a significant effect on your financial situation. Buying a house is often the biggest transaction of your life, and it helps if you can continue to live in the house after you've bought it. When you're young you usually live in quite primitive accommodation, but as time passes and, one hopes, your financial situation becomes more sound, your standard of living rises. The bookcase made of three planks and a few bricks is exchanged for an IKEA bookcase Billy; and when your finances improve even more you invest in an IKEA bookcase Bonde. Your home becomes bigger and more elegant, but later, when more years have passed, your home might become smaller as you reach old age. You might end up in a "care home", i.e. a large building full of old people. In these homes pensioners spend all their time exchanging medicines and diagnoses, and in the evenings there are parties where the wine flows free and promiscuity knows no bounds. Or at least, that's how it ought to be. You deserve a bit of fun and some carefree pleasures when you are getting on in years and have ended up in a residence with a highly suspect name like a "care home".

Interests
and
Hobbies

"Are you saying that the whole family was shocked when your ninety-five-year-old father died?"

"Yes, we were."

"But he was ninety-five after all. Why were you shocked?"

"Because his parachute didn't open."

The above exchange demonstrates that interests and hobbies don't need to be age-related. Which hobbies are linked with age? Should seventy-five-year-olds be allowed to play hockey and video games? Or does that seem odd? Should you paint tin soldiers or make lace when you're thirty? How old do you have to be before you can do crochet work? Interests and hobbies generally do change as you grow older. What you were interested in and spent your leisure time doing when you were twenty is usually not as exciting and interesting when you are fifty. Are you regarded as strange if you have what are regarded as interests unsuitable for your age? If you are seventy and are mad about hip-hop? If you are sixty and want to go to a disco wearing tight-fitting clothes and with a bare midriff? If you are twenty-five and like playing bingo? Or if you think like the man who said: "I've had the same interests all my life. When I was twenty-five I liked beer and young women of my own age, and now that I'm seventy I still like beer and twenty-five-year-old girls."

There are hobbies that are totally independent of age. Bird-watching, for instance, is suitable for all ages. It is just as cold and boring no matter what age you are, standing in a swamp at five in the morning hoping to catch a glimpse of a blue-eared crested finch. (Or just as exciting and enjoyable, irrespective of age, if that's the way you see it). Seeing a blue-eared crested finch is pretty big deal in any case. Especially if it's a female with their characteristic miaowing and grunting. (Female crested finches are often animal imitators).

Stamp collecting is also suitable for all ages. Coming across an unfranked pale green Albanian jubilee issue with irregular perforations is bliss for both a twenty-year-old and an eighty-year-old. But one shouldn't collect stamps in front of an open window. Many people (mostly men) like electric trains. It's perfectly permissible to play with electric trains when you are ten, and when you are seventy-five. At ages in between, it is regarded as slightly dodgy. (Unless you are a train driver). The advantage with being a little older, as far as hobbies and interests are concerned, is that a bit of eccentricity is more acceptable. As an old man you can devote yourself to peculiar activities and indulge your eccentricities without people reacting so much. "Now ancient Grandad's up in the attic skiing again. I hope he doesn't ski into ancient Grandma's chicken coop again."

An important question with regard to age and leisure-time activities is: Do you have to start playing golf at some point in your forties or fifties? Is it prescribed by law? And if so, why? We all know what golfers are like. There are two kinds of people: those who play golf and those who don't. The problem is that they are often married to each other. There are golfers of all ages, but if you haven't started playing golf earlier, you are expected to take it up in your middle age. Another interest that generally blossoms forth in the same age group is wine. For some reason people aged around fifty are supposed to take up an interest in wine. (Instead of football? Instead of sex? Why?) It used to be enough simply to drink wine, but now you have to talk wine. In the old days some wines were good, others were less good and a few were extremely good. Now terms like "good" and "less good" are no longer used. Nowadays wines have "a smokey tone of ripe gorgonzola with a hint of bonfires", or they are "robust and slightly ironic without being cheerfully strenuous". You also need to know what type of grapes have been trampled to bits to make this wine, and if the grapes have come from a vine in clay-rich soil or soil-rich clay. Why do you need to know that? It's not so easy to answer that question, but perhaps it is good to know such things. If you do, you have something to talk to your friends about. Could it be that by the time you reach your fifties you have exhausted all topics of conversation with your friends and acquaintances, and need to find something else to talk about? Wines are an excellent topic. However, it assumes that everybody taking part in the conversation has the same interest.

"Last Saturday I tasted a fantastic Alsace wine with an indivisible nutty taste with hints of burnt lemon marmalade."

"I've also tasted that one! A terrific wine, a touch of subtle honey salt in the aftertaste. And an almost rectangular feeling of vanilla."

"Exactly! Have you also tasted it, Kevin?"
"I generally belch quite a lot if I drink beer."

When you get to that age and hence have just taken up both golf and the appreciation of wine, you must be careful not to mix up the concepts. When you try to hang on in there when conversing with your friends who are mad about both golf and wine, your nervousness might cause you to make mistakes.

"Yes indeed, a really good wine with a sliced aftertaste but a good handicap. This wine would go well with game, or birdies as I usually call them. At the third hole last Sunday I managed to sink a real Bordeaux, but then I landed in a medium dry bunker with a corked taste. I didn't know whether to take the seven iron or a somewhat lighter chardonnay with hints of apple to get out of it. – I collect stamps as well."

A New
Partner

A lot of people change partners as they make their way through life. There are of course a few couples who come together at the age of fifteen and stay together until they die; but most people have several partners on their journey through life. When are you too old to change partners, or to find a new one? Is there ever a time when you are too old for that? Are you ever too old to split up?

There's a story about a very old couple – he was ninety-seven and she was ninety-five. They had been married for over seventy years, and had now decided to get divorced. Their friends couldn't believe their ears. "What?" they said. "Getting divorced? At your age?! You must be mad! You've been married for over seventy years and now you're talking about getting divorced, when you're almost a hundred!"

"Well," the old couple responded, "we've been talking about a divorce for many years now, but we wanted to wait until the children were dead."

One is probably never too old to start living with a new partner. There are endless examples of people who have begun living together after their seventieth or eightieth birthdays. Do you become younger if you start living with a much younger partner? Or do you feel unusually old because your partner is so young and may have different interests and values from your own? There are relationships between people of very different ages when the older person has complained that his new sweetheart has never heard of the Beatles. "The Beatles! She doesn't know who the Beatles were! I couldn't believe my ears. She knew about 'that old codger McCartney', but that was all. When I

wondered how it was possible not to have heard of the Beatles, she asked me if I knew about... I can't remember what they were called, some rock band I've never heard of. I wonder how this is going to turn out."

Naturally there can be problems if the age difference in a relationship leads to a conflict of interests. If one of the partners want to go to ice hockey practice while the other wants to go to a meeting at the Old People's Club, this can lead to disagreements. Woody Allen is said to have complained (when he was well into middle age) because his then girlfriend didn't have time to spend with him because she had to go home and do her homework. If a relationship like that lasts, those involved can always console themselves with the thought that the difference in age is less noticeable, the older you grow. It's much more of a problem when the partners are eighteen and forty than when they are eighty and a hundred-and-two.

There can also be problems when you meet your partner's friends who are about the same age as he or she is. They may not have the same degree of tolerance and understanding of the big age gap as your sweetheart does. When an older man meets the friends of his younger girlfriend, he might well feel uncomfortable, wrongly dressed, and that he is using the wrong jargon. And he also risks hearing remarks

such as: "Why have you brought your dad along with you? What? It isn't your dad? You mean you're living with him?! Come on, you're pulling my leg!" And when the younger woman meets the friends of her older lover, it's just the same. She feels uncomfortable, wrongly dressed, and that she is using the wrong jargon. And she might well hear comments such as: "So this is your daughter, eh? No? You mean it's your... Well, well! Do the authorities know about this?"

How big an age gap is "socially acceptable"? That depends on the circles in which you move. It also depends on who is the older partner. For some reason it is more acceptable if the man is considerably older than the woman. If the woman is twenty years older than her boyfriend, a lot of people shake their heads and mutter something about "baby-snatching".

But irrespective of how old you are, it's natural for you to want to be together with somebody. It doesn't matter if you are twenty-seven or fifty-seven. And if you are fifty-seven and want to be together with somebody who is twenty-seven, that's OK as long as the twenty-seven-year-old is all for it as well. (It's also possible that the twenty-seven-year-old is actually fifty-two – see the chapter on plastic surgery.)

Friends

Generally speaking, we keep changing our friends as the years go by. Why is that? Why do we have so few childhood friends left when we become adults? It's probably due to the fact that what held those friendships together when we were children or teenagers no longer has the same significance when we are grown up. Perhaps we played sport together, discovered the opposite sex together, swotted for exams together – all the kind of things that cemented our friendship while we were growing up. But then, all of a sudden, we are grown up, and different friendship factors become important. Intellectual differences also become more noticeable when we are adult. The boy next door, whom we admired for his daring, agility and sporting skills, turns out to have the same level of intelligence as a moderately gifted chimpanzee. (No wonder he was so good at climbing up trees and was so fond of bananas.)

Some people don't want to meet their childhood friends because they don't want to be seen now as they were then. Podgy Pete, who was so hopeless at sport and scared of girls and was known as "Piggy", doesn't want to meet his childhood friends for obvious reasons. Nowadays Podgy Pete is a chartered accountant, no longer fat, and happily married to Anna. But when he meets his old friends in town, they shout: "Hi there Piggy, how's things? Met any nice bits of skirt recently?" Who can blame the former Podgy Pete for preferring new friends, friends who regard him as a chartered accountant of normal weight with a pretty wife?

There can also be a total reversal of the roles ascribed to friends as one grows older. "The failure", the wimp whom nobody bothered about or just made fun of, has turned into somebody entirely different, while "Lucky Len", who was popular, handsome and clever, has become an insignificant nobody.

Chekhov has portrayed brilliantly a meeting between two childhood friends, one of whom has been successful and carved out a brilliant career for himself – but the other one doesn't know this until they've been talking for a while. When he hears the impressive title his childhood friend has acquired and realises his standing in society, he changes his attitude completely and becomes an obsequious underling. We understand that neither of them have any desire to meet again. We all change with the passage of time, and if we and our friends develop in different ways, it's only natural that strong childhood friendships loosen up and are blown away by the winds of time.

An increasingly wide social gap can thus affect friendships. Ollie and Jimmy are best friends – they come from different social backgrounds, to be sure, but that doesn't matter. Not when they are young, that is. The years pass and Ollie becomes rich and successful, lives in a large mansion and drives a car that costs about as much as a luxurious

holiday cottage with its own private beach. Jimmy hasn't done nearly as well for himself. He is neither rich nor successful, and his car only starts when it's pointing down a hill. When Ollie and his family go to the Maldives on holiday, Jimmy and his family try to find a hill so that they can start the car and drive to the packed public beach just outside town. When Ollie and Jimmy meet and start talking about what they've been doing on their holidays, they both find it rather painful and find themselves squirming in embarrassment.

"You know, the Maldives are not really all that marvellous. The water is nice and clean and warm, but Louise cut her foot while walking on the beach."

"Oh dear, I'm sorry to hear that. We also did quite a bit of swimming last summer. It wasn't exactly the Maldives, but it was fifteen degrees in the water at most – Nancy got frostbite in her toes."

Some friends disappear as time passes even though they haven't emigrated to Australia or been banished by your partner. In some strange way the friendship subsides and runs slowly away into the sand. Although there have been no confrontations nor outside influences, the friendship gradually fades away and dies, and nobody really knows why. How can somebody you've been so close to for so many years suddenly vanish more or less totally from your consciousness? "What on earth happened to Bobby? I haven't seen him for several years. We used to be great friends. But then he disappeared and I don't know what happened to him. I ought to phone him and find out how he's getting on."

Of course you should. But you don't. It remains a passing thought that never has the strength to develop from thought into action. Time has wiped away all the traces in the sand of the friendship that once existed. Life goes on, we grow older – but what happened to Bobby?

At what age do friends disappear to be replaced by new ones? This keeps on happening throughout our lives. New friends can turn up at any moment, and old friends can vanish just as suddenly at any time. Is it possible to acquire new friends when you are getting on in years? Or have you settled down into roles and habits that consciously or unconsciously build a protective wall that is not so easy to penetrate? Of course you can make new friends when you are older, even if it's probably easier to do so when you are younger. In your younger days you are more open and unreserved, and haven't yet locked yourself into habits and roles. You offer more of yourself to others and are more spontaneous, which makes it easier to form friendships. It can also be more difficult to find new friends when you are older because by that time most people already have a circle of friends and are not all that interested in acquiring new ones. It's easier when you are a child, meet a new playmate and after ten minutes of being together ask: "Do you want to be my best friend?" If you were to ask the same question of somebody you'd met ten minutes earlier when you are grown up, you would probably be regarded as stark staring mad.

Your need for friends varies according to your age (and of course your individual needs depend on the type of person you are). When you are twenty, you might well want to have friends you can party with, and discuss the big questions of life.

"What really is the meaning of life, eh? I mean, its basic meaning, as it were. Eh? What's the point of living? Is there no red wine left? Surely there was another bottle, wasn't there? Who's taken it? Does life have any meaning at all?"

When you are thirty, it helps if your friends are in the same phase as you are yourself – otherwise there will be no real dialogue, just two monologues.

"Last night I was at the wickedest party the world has ever seen. There were three bits of skirt who flashed their knickers at me – I think two of them were sisters. And the music was enough to knock the shit out of you."

"Little Josh was sick twice this morning. It looked a bit pale green, but maybe that was the mashed peas he'd been eating."

"I sank a hell of a lot of whisky – single malt, not too peaty. It tasted top bollock. Cost a bloody fortune as well."

"Little Josh had a touch of diarrhoea also, but it wasn't pale green, more light brown."

"Ugh, how disgusting! What are you on about?"

When we are in our fifties we like to have friends with whom we can discuss the various pains that are starting to afflict us, and in our sixties we might well want to exchange boasts and exploits of our

grandchildren. But no matter how old we are, we want to have the feeling that our friends like us, and care about us and our lives. If we still have childhood friends when we are elderly, we can amuse ourselves by asking how many of those friends would become our friends if we were to meet them now for the first time. Deadly dull Betty, who's been our friend for the last thirty years – what would we think of her if we met her today for the first time? We would think that she was a very nice lady, but totally lacking in charm and so boring that all the clocks stop when she enters a room. And Stan, who's been telling us jokes for the last twenty-five years (the same jokes), jokes that he's the only one who laughs at – what would we think about him if we'd only just met him? An inoffensive but rather trying type – would we really make friends with him today? Or boastful Susan – how long would we put up with her if she entered out lives now? Not to mention Cliff, who we thought was so charming but unreliable? He's still unreliable, but is he still charming?

So why did we like them so much, all those years ago? And why are we still friends with boring Betty and trying Stan? Perhaps both we and our friends have changed as the years have passed. We didn't think that Betty was so boring when we first met her thirty years ago. (And no doubt she wasn't.) She has become more boring as the years have passed, and perhaps we have changed our preferences. So why do we still socialise with Betty, Stan, Susan and all the others? Probably for several reasons. A mixture of convenience, routine, and a feeling of ingrained security that induces us to continue meeting

these old friends. It's convenient – it wouldn't be all that easy to go out looking for new friends. And of course there's an element of routine – the friendship has lasted for so long that it has become a habit, and you don't break off habits so easily. And no matter what, it feels quite comforting and confidence-inspiring to hang on to these friends we know so well. (Even if it is hard to laugh at Stan's old jokes when you hear them for the fifty-eleventh time.)

Plastic
Surgery

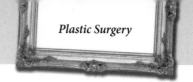
Are you thinking of undergoing plastic surgery? Just a little bit. "A minor cosmetic procedure", as they say. If so, why? To make yourself more attractive? To become younger? Would an operation like that make you younger? Will you live longer if you have a few bags and wrinkles removed from your face?

In the old days it was only female film stars who had cosmetic surgery. (This should not be confused with all the plastic surgery performed for medical reasons in order to correct deformities, or to heal burns etc.) Then it was the turn of male film stars – perhaps they could prolong their careers at the top of the heap if they looked a bit younger. It wasn't possible to play the first lover of the young heroine if you looked as if you'd just celebrated your eighty-fifth birthday. Nowadays you don't need to be a film star in order to undergo plastic surgery. All kinds of people, of both sexes, do it. When you have so many wrinkles on your forehead that you have to screw your hat on, you might well feel that it's time for "a minor cosmetic procedure". The wrinkles disappear, the double chin is taken away and the bags under your eyes are removed. You want ears that protrude less and breasts that protrude more? Nothing is impossible for a skilful plastic surgeon.

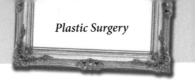

Plastic Surgery

Are there any disadvantages in undergoing cosmetic surgery? Can anything go wrong? Something can always go wrong, and there is no guarantee that the result will be as good as you had hoped for. After a face lift, your face has a tendency to look rather taut and inflexible. In that case do you look younger, or do you look like a mummy thawed out in the microwave? If the skin is too taut your eyebrows will rise up every time you smile, and your eyelids will close every time you yawn. This can have a somewhat bewildering effect on those around you. When you smile your eyebrows rise up and you look surprised. Surprised at what? And when you talk you automatically wink and blink all the time. Everybody you talk to will wonder why you look so surprised and keep winking at them.

If you have silicone inserted into your body, there is a risk that the silicone might start moving. A woman who wanted an "apple-shaped" bottom had two large silicon implants inserted into her buttocks. The implants later wandered down the back of her legs and ended up in her calves. Her calves made her look as if she were the Olympic 100-metres champion and had won the title with the aid of anabolic steroids. Her bottom looked like a rather sad pear. Having an operation doesn't necessarily ensure that you will become prettier or younger.

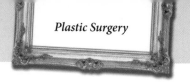

When it comes to cosmetic interventions, there are alternatives to operations. A plastic surgeon does not rely on knives alone, but has access to some interesting injections as well. He can inject Botox to incapacitate small nerves so that your muscles slacken off and the wrinkles are ironed out. Doesn't it sound tempting, injecting some nerve poison into your face? Well worth it in order to look a bit younger? The cosmetic surgeon can also inject collagen to give you thicker lips, if you think your lips are too thin and think that thin lips are a sign of increasing age. Of course, a good surgeon can work wonders in other areas of your body as well as your face. It's not only noses, chins, wrinkles and bags that can be adjusted and improved: other parts of the body can be adjusted. Women's breasts can be made to change both their size and shape, and bottoms, calves and stomachs can also be altered. Some men have operations performed on a part of their bodies to make it longer or thicker (no, not their arms), and both men and women undergo liposuction of their stomachs in order to take a weight off their minds.

At what age do you have cosmetic surgery? That depends on the reason for having the operation. Younger people have operations in order to become better looking and more attractive. They want to have adjustments made to their breasts, lips and noses, for instance, in the hope of coming closer to their ideal of beauty. When you are older it is generally rejuvenation you have in the back of your mind when you ring the cosmetic surgeon's doorbell. You think it's time to get rid of wrinkles, folds and extra chins. You want the crows feet ironing out

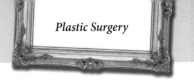

and the bags removed. You are looking forward to the scalpel cutting away twenty years from your face and body. The fount of youth has transmogrified into a sharp knife.

If, with the help of a cosmetic surgeon, you end up looking younger (rather than a warmed-up mummy), will you also be younger inside? Do we feel younger if we think we look younger? Well, it's possible, for a time at least. But do we become younger mentally? For instance, do we have a better memory and faster reflexes if we have our double chins and those enormous bags under our eyes removed? Of course not, but some people might be satisfied by the feeling that they have outwitted the mirror. If you have spent a lot of time before the operation looking into the mirror, sighing sadly and saying: "Good Lord, how old I look," you can hope that you'll feel happier when you look in the mirror after the operation. Then you might say: "Good Lord, don't I look young? And surprised. Why are my eyebrows going up like that?"

If you are lucky, it might be possible to deceive the mirror and people you meet after acquiring a rejuvenated appearance by artificial means, but the question is: how far can you deceive yourself? A much simpler and cheaper way of conjuring away at least some of the signs of ageing is to wear a large, dark pair of sun glasses. They will hide the crows

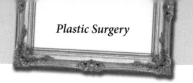

feet and bags around your eyes. If you want to take this poor man's approach to rejuvenation a step further, you can take to wearing a wide-brimmed floppy hat, which will cover up any grey or thinning hair. By means of these simple aids you can become much younger for very little outlay, and at the same time you will acquire a hint of Greta Garbo about you. If you think you are not concealing enough of the devastation wreaked by the ageing process with the aid of large sun glasses and a hat, you could instead wear a large bag over your face. Then nobody will be able to see your crows feet, chins, wrinkles etc, but there is a risk that people might look at you anyway, even if you wear a bag that is discreet in both shape and colour. People will look at you in surprise and think: "Why has he got a bag over his head? He must be a bit odd. I wonder how old he is."

If you are scared of doctors, scalpels and surgery, instead of cosmetic surgery you could opt instead for "rejuvenation creams" in order to look younger. There are quite a few such creams that promise the most amazing results. According to the adverts, these creams and salves remove wrinkles, cellulite and unnecessary concentrations of fat in an almost miraculous way. The more cream you rub into your face, the younger you become. The ingredients in these creams are often very exclusive. The advertising material informs us that they are made from unborn bee larvae, Japanese honey flower jelly and ground rosebud aroma. Especially the latter is difficult to source. Not only do these creams make you free of wrinkles, but they also "restore to your skin its youthful elasticity and gentle freshness". The creams are

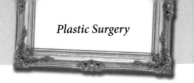

usually incredibly expensive, but who worries about money when you have the opportunity of restoring to your skin its "youthful elasticity"?

At what age should one start smearing one's face with unborn bee larvae and Japanese honeyflower jelly? The makers of these products say that you should start when you are twenty-five or so. "To keep your face young," it says in the adverts. How young? And why? Do these creams help? To do what? Do they make you younger? If you start using them at the age of twenty-five, can you count on growing very old and still look as if you were twenty-five for the whole of your life? And if that is so, might it not seem a little odd in some circumstances? Imaging standing there looking as if you are twenty-five, surrounded by your children who both are and look as if they're in their forties. (Why don't your children use these creams? If they did, at least you'd all look the same age.) Not to mention when you try to use your senior citizen's bus pass. "What kind of ticket is this?! Do you really think I'm going to let you board this bus with that? Go and buy a school pupil's ticket and stop trying to be funny!"

If you go to a plastic surgeon because you think you look old and want to change that, it could be a good idea to take a closer look at the surgeon. How old does the plastic surgeon look? How old does his spouse look? Do they look old? If so, why? Shouldn't they look

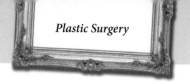

young?! Or do they look young? Perhaps they are young! Ask them how old they are, and see if their real age corresponds to how old they look. A good plastic surgeon should preferably be quite old (in which case he or she ought to be skilled and experienced, while it's still possible to control the shaking of the hand), but he or she ought to look young. Cosmetic surgeons who specialise in "rejuvenation surgery" obviously ought to look like walking advertisements for their profession. Devoid of wrinkles and looking good, they should rise awkwardly from their chair, knees creaking, and say: "I can fit your operation in next month – in fact it will be the last one I perform before I retire."

How do you
**Make the Right
Decisions?**

Somebody said: "Living means making decisions."

For the whole of our lives, we are forced to make decisions. We constantly find ourselves in situations where a choice must be made, or at a crossroads where we have to decide which direction we should take. Even as children we have to make choices.

"You can only have one slice of cake. Do you want the one with raspberry jam or the one with vanilla cream?"

"I want both."

"No, you can only have one. Which is it to be?"

This is a recurrent dilemma, even when we are adults: we "want both". And even if we can't have both, we still want to have our cake and eat it. That isn't possible either. All the time we have to decide what we want to do.

"You can't both be married and live as if you were single! I said before we got married that there would be no cooling-off period, or right of return!"

At what age do we start looking back and wondering if we made the right decision in various situations? When we're thirty? Should we have chosen another profession? It's still not too late to re-train.

When we're forty? Have we chosen the wrong career? The wrong marriage partner? The wrong parents?

When we're fifty? Have we chosen the wrong sort of life? The wrong life style? The wrong tie?

Or do we have to wait until we're sixty before we start thinking about the wrong decisions we have made in our lives? When it's time

to glance back over our shoulders and wonder if we ought to start fretting? Or perhaps look in the rear-view mirror and feel pretty satisfied with the choices we've made. Is there any point, irrespective of our age, in sitting down and thinking about what might have been, if we'd taken a different route when we came to a crossroads in life? Ought we to have been a mite more cautious before investing our life's savings in drilling for oil in our back garden? Should we have been more adventurous that time and gone in for a life as an ostrich farmer instead of becoming a state-registered auditor?

Should we not have checked the rubber band before embarking on our bungy-jump?

Different ages place us in different situations where a choice must be made. Some decisions are more important than others. Choosing our education and profession, selecting a partner, a house, a car, a telephone operating company, a pension fund, a make of jeans (low-slung waist and flared legs, or flared waist and low-slung legs?) There is an infinite number of decisions we make, and then wonder afterwards if we've made the right one. The only one we are unable to decide about is the direction the lift is going in when we die. Up or down? We'll find out eventually. Meanwhile, we have to get on with life, choose, choose, choose, and then pester our brains with questions about whether we've made the right decisions. There are so many choices we could find ourselves regretting:

"I ought to have accepted that job with Dibnah & Sons, I could have made a decent career for myself there. I could have risen to the top of the company. I could have been the 'Sons' if I'd done a decent job. I signed up for the firm Iron & Scrap instead. Who wants to be 'Scrap'?"

"I ought to have picked Sally-Jo instead of Mary-Jane. Sally-Jo is pretty, rich, pleasant and clever. Mary-Jane's just the opposite. But she was the only one who'd have me. Who said there was freedom of choice and free will? The philosophers are wrong, there's no such thing as free will."

"I should have taken the night-school course in IT instead of origami. Who's interested in anybody with a Higher National in Origami? What kind of a job can you get with qualifications like that? The only thing potential employers ask about is if I'm computer literate. When I tell them that I can turn seven sheets of white paper into a Chinese junk, they just give me a queer look. I once took some sheets of paper from the Human Resources Manager's desk while he was interviewing me, and made them into a Japanese temple. Guess if he offered me a job. I should have gone in for IT."

How do you Make the Right Decisions?

"I ought to have bet on Red Devil in the seventh race. It was a choice between Red Devil and Peg-Leg Pete, and I went for Peg-Leg Pete. Not a good choice. The blasted pony came last, way behind the rest. I ought to have realised that it wasn't going to win, if only I'd looked at it a bit more closely. I mean, it's not often you see a three-legged racehorse."

"I should have emigrated to America and become a millionaire. I chose between that and staying at home. I'd made up my mind to emigrate and was due to go the American Embassy to collect the emigration papers, but it was raining and I'd only just been to the hairdresser's and so I didn't want to go out. I thought I could just as well go the next day, but it was raining then as well and so I never got round to it. Just think how different your life can turn out, depending on the decisions you make. If it hadn't been raining, I'd have been a millionaire in America now."

"I ought to have got myself a better alibi. It was stupid to say I was round at the neighbour's all evening. I actually chose to say that rather than claiming I was at home in bed. I thought it sounded better to say that I was at the neighbour's. I ought to have realised that the police would check up with the neighbour. Obviously, the neighbour told them the truth and said that I wasn't there. I don't know him at all. Next time I'll think before making a decision. But prison food's not bad at all. It was fish and chips last night, it was very good."

One of the disadvantages of growing older is that you think it's too late to do certain things. It feels as if the train has left and you don't get a second chance. You made the wrong decision some time ago, and now it's too late to change anything. Why did you make the decision you did? Now, looking back, you might well be able to see why you ought to have made a different decision; but now you have the benefit of hindsight. It's not difficult to see which horse you should have placed a bet on after the race is over. How fruitful is it to speculate about what might have been if only you'd made a different decision? When you made that choice, you presumably did so on the basis of what you knew and felt at that time. Now, ten or twenty years on, you might know and feel differently; but you can hardly take that as justification for making the wrong decision when you actually made it. (Obviously, there are clear cases of having made a wrong decision that you can identify very soon after the event. Such as betting on Peg-Leg Pete in the seventh race.) It could be that chance (whatever that means) plays a part in the decisions we take. Chance or coincidence can sometimes dictate what we choose to do. Sometimes chance is just as good at making choices as we are ourselves.

Is it certain that things would have turned out better if we'd made a different choice? Is it certain the man who married Mary-Jane instead of Sally-Jo would have been any happier if he'd married Sally-Jo instead? Sally-Jo might have turned out to be an alcoholic, been notoriously unfaithful, and squeezed the toothpaste tube in the middle. And would the man who placed a bet on Peg-Leg Pete in the seventh race have led a better life if he'd placed his money on Red Devil instead? Red Devil won and the punters who backed him won loadsa money at odds of 32-1. What would have happened if he'd won? He would have resigned his job and gone in for betting on horses full-time. It wouldn't have taken him long to gamble away his house and belongings and become a pauper. He'd have ended up as a park-bench drop-out with everything he possessed in a couple of torn Woolworth's carrier bags. It might be as well to recognize that things might not necessarily have turned out any better if we'd decided differently from the way we did.

And so we don't need to fret when we are a bit older and worried about whether we've made the right decisions. There's nothing to say that things would have turned out any better if we'd decided otherwise. Perhaps we have a sort of instinctive, inbuilt emotional compass that leads us to make the right decisions more often than not. Einstein once said: "We should assert our reason when we make minor and fairly minor decisions; but when it comes to the major decisions we should leave it to our emotions." Perhaps we automatically choose with our emotions when there's an important decision to be made. And with our reason when we place a bet on Peg -Leg Pete in the seventh race.

Jobs
and
Careers

What happens to your job, and your possible career, as the years go by? Is your career heading in the right direction? Or the wrong direction? Or isn't it going in any direction at all? How long do you have "future prospects"? When is your working future behind you? At a certain age you say: "Now I've come as far as I'm going to get, I'm not going to progress any further." And then you stand still on the career ladder, or slide slowly downwards.

Is there an approximate age limit when continuous promotion comes to a stop? That depends of course on what your job is. If you are a professional footballer or ice hockey player, there would be no point in your reckoning on a brilliant career after you've turned forty. (There are exceptions, it's true, but very few.) But if you are an artist, for instance, or a carpenter, or a doctor, you might well produce your best work when you are sixty, seventy or even older.

Can you start a new career at any age? (Probably not as a footballer, but in some other profession.) If you are forty or fifty and think you are not going to progress any further in the job you are doing, can you take up something else? – Of course you can, why not? (But perhaps not as an ice hockey player.)

Is it important to have a career? To keep on being promoted in the work you are doing, is that necessary? Yes, it is for some people. You might ask yourself why this should be so, but it is. But what if you've never had a career? That's OK as well. It's not written in stone anywhere that the point and meaning of life is to make a career, earn a lot of money or acquire posh titles.

It's often more difficult to get a job when you grow older. Why? By then you are cleverer and more experienced – shouldn't you be a more attractive proposition in the labour market?

No.

Why not?

Because that's the way it is.

Next question. Do you have to be young in order to get certain jobs? Which ones? Which are the jobs where you aren't allowed to be old? Ones which are dedicated to the demands of young people. But Mick Jagger isn't all that young and he makes a living as a rock singer. How does he manage that? And the guitarist Keith Richards in the Rolling Stones looks as if he's been dead for several years, but he is working very successfully in a field where you are considered to be old when you are thirty. So when are you "too old"? Too old for what?

Are there perhaps any jobs in which it's an advantage to be a bit older? Would you like to be operated on by a twenty-three-year-old surgeon? Or would you prefer a fifty-five-year-old? Would you want the pilot of the plane you are boarding to look as if he has just left school? (With pretty poor A-level results into the bargain.) Or would you feel better if your pilot was middle-aged and had lots of gold bars on his uniform?

Sometimes it's good to be young, and sometimes it´s an advantage if someone else is a bit older.

Spare Parts

"I'm so old now that I have to put my false teeth in and switch on my hearing aid before I can ask if anybody knows where I've left my glasses."

The above quotation shows that as we grow older, we might need various aids and spare parts in order to make life easier to cope with. In this day and age we have access to various aids that didn't exist in the old days. Nowadays, for instance, it's easy to have an operation to fit a pacemaker in patients with heart problems. "Show me somebody with a song in his heart, and I'll show you somebody who can tune in to Radio Caroline on his pacemaker."

There are so many spare parts available nowadays that we can make use of whenever necessary. Perhaps the commonest of them is spectacles. As we grow older, most of us need reading glasses – in fact we need three pairs: one to use at home, one at work, and another for when we are looking for the other pairs. A characteristic of reading glasses is that they are always vanishing, and they are never where we were quite sure we had left them. When some people reach a certain age, they attach their reading glasses to a cord that goes round their necks; others say they prefer to lose them and keep fumbling their way through life rather than resorting to a "senility string".

A lot of people don't want to acknowledge that they have reached an age when they need spectacles. They screw up their eyes, read only the headlines in the newspapers, and refuse to buy glasses. It's only when they've misread price labels in shops several times and discovered when they come to the cash desk that the jacket didn't cost £65 but £428, that they reluctantly invest in a pair of reading glasses. Obviously, they lose their new spectacles shortly after buying them, and have to buy a new pair in order to find the others.

Another reason for capitulating and accepting that you really do need spectacles is that you can't read the dosage on the labels of your medicine bottles. It's true of course that a lot of people take their medicines whenever they feel like it (see the chapter *Health*), but it can be interesting to know when the doctor intended his patient to take the tablets. "Does it say take one tablet four times a day? Or does it say one tablet every four days? Or is that an eight? It looks like a little cat. Maybe I ought to get myself some glasses."

It's not only your sight that changes as the years pass. Your teeth are also affected by the ravages of time. You may need new teeth in the form of jacket crowns, titanium teeth or dentures. Or perhaps your own teeth are still sound but have changed colour and are no longer as white as they used to be. It's possible to have your teeth bleached, or thin, white porcelain plates can be attached to them – which is better, if more expensive, than brushing them with Tippex.

Spare parts include hearing aids, hip joint replacements for worn-out hips, artificial knee joints for worn-out knees, and penis extensions in the form of a Porsche Carrera. It's presumably just a matter of time before it becomes possible to replace people's brains. This is really something to look forward to. We'll be able to exchange our tired brain with its bad memory for a new agile one full of good ideas and with a memory like a computer. Brains that have never been used (and previously belonged to politicians) will be a bit more expensive, of course, but not all that much because their memory is so short. We shan't need to exchange all our brain, just the parts we think could do with freshening up. A new memory, a few new ideas and a few improper fantasies are what we need when we are getting on in years, to make us feel young at heart again. And with the help of our new, improved memory, we might even be able to remember where we left our reading glasses.

Having children makes you grow older. The old saying: "Grey hair is hereditary, you can get it from your children" sums it up rather well. The age of the children also affects how old you feel yourself. If you have older children, it's not so easy to convince yourself that you are still a teenager. When people ask you: "How old are your children?", you may well be tempted to tell a white lie. "Er... they are three and five," you say, thinking that is what they were very recently. But "the three-year-old" has just taken her A-levels and the "five-year-old" is at university. If you're lucky there won't be any follow-up questions, but you are not lucky.

"Three and five years old? I thought somebody said you had children who've just taken their A-levels."

"Er... yes, that's true. It's little Milly – she's very advanced for her age."

Another way round it, if you don't want to tell lies about the age of your children, is to doctor the truth about yourself slightly, so as not to seem so old.

"So, you have grown-up children, do you?"

"Yes, but I became a father very early on. I was only four when I had the first one."

It makes no difference how young you feel or look, grown-up children make you seem elderly. The film star Cary Grant's mother didn't like the fact that her son had white hair. "Having a white-haired son makes me feel so old," she said. She was turned ninety at the time.

Grandchildren make you realise even more starkly how old you are yourself. It can be difficult to feel young if you have grandchildren. (Unless of course you are twenty-eight and have grown up in an environment where nobody has heard of family planning.) The word "granddad" evokes somebody very old with a long white beard, while the title "grandma" is associated with a little white-haired lady who makes apple pies and has pains in her knees. But these outdated associations don't work any more. Today's granddad or grandma are often active people who sometimes want to fly to Marbella and play golf rather than being babysitters and changing nappies. Modern grandparents are fully occupied with work, sailing, playing tennis or going to the pub. Besides, Granddad often has small children of his own, acquired in the autumn of his life as a result of his new marriage to Betty (aged twenty-six).

If you don't know whether it's the parents or grandparents sitting and babbling with a little child, it's easy to work it out. You only need to see how they handle the child. If they just sit there with an idiot smile on their lips, and let it do whatever it likes, they are looking after their grandchild. If they grow irritated and snarl at it when it pours milk into its hair, they are the child's parents. Granddad allows the kid to hammer nails into the piano and make chalk drawings on the silk wallpaper (unless he's a very old-fashioned grandfather who thinks children should be raised in a reformatory). There is also a difference between how parents and grandparents deal with a small child who refuses to eat its food. The parents yell: "If you don't eat up that food, you won't get any afters!" or "Eat it all now or you'll go straight to

bed!" If the parents are sufficiently tired and irritated, they roar: "Eat up that bloody food or we'll dump you in the woods and leave you for the wolves – they always eat up everything!"

But the grandparents take a softy-softly approach instead. "Come on, have a little bit and then we can have some ice cream." If the child still refuses to eat, Grandma or Granddad eats the food when nobody's looking, and then they say to the child' parents: "Look, little Johnny's eaten up everything, so now he can have some chocolate pudding for being such a good boy!"

Have you ever thought about what kind of idiots buy horrendously expensive designer clothes for little kids? Which halfwit pays a small fortune for a tiny little jumper the little brat will have grown out of inside two months? Well, the child's grandparents do. When you see a one-year-old in a Dior dress or a two-year-old in a double-breasted Armani suit, you know it's a present from Granddad or Grandma. Needless to say, the little kid is only too pleased to be able to dribble and be sick all over designer clothes – it gives an extra dimension to both the dribbling and the vomiting.

Somebody once said: "There's only one perfect child in this world of ours – and all mothers have it."

It's even more true to say: "There's only one perfect grandchild in this world of ours – and all grandmas and granddads have it."

Masks

The masks we put on or start to wear when we are young can turn stiff and be difficult to take off when we are older. Masks that stay in place for too long can get stuck and there is a risk that they will become permanent. There are a lot of different masks we can adopt. The constantly smiling and cheerful mask is not all that unusual. We think (and it may well be true) that we'll be well-liked and popular if we are always merry and bright. Besides, it enables us to conceal what we really think and how we feel.

"Hi! How are things? Everything's fine here! Life is great! Everything's terrific! What's that? How are things at work? Oh, great! I got the sack last week, it feels good. All's well at home. We're getting divorced and little Eric's started on drugs, it feels marvellous. By the way, I heard a really funny joke the other day that I just have to tell you. There was this priest and a nun…"

Some people choose a solemn mask in an attempt to seem intellectual, clever or serious. No fooling about here. A solemn mask that informs all and sundry that they are dealing with a person of intelligence and culture, combined with a touch of discerning melancholy that only deep thinkers can attain.

"Hello there. Have you read Arthur Krossenschlüger's latest book, *It Hurts When I Breathe*? It really is a superb bifocal depiction with eclectic contemplation of the anatomy of suffering. I have a pain in my foot as well."

Masks

There are people who assume a martyr's mask even when they are young. They think: people might not want to like me, but at least they can feel sorry for me. A feel-sorry-for-me mask can turn stiff quite quickly, and anybody wearing one risks going through life carrying a large sign that says "Feel sorry for me! All the time!" Every question about how things are is answered by a torrent of words and much sighing. The opening sentence is always: "Not all that good, I'm afraid," and it's downhill all the way from there. The martyr's mask is not the type of mask that will bring social popularity.

The masks we put on when we're young might well need changing when we are older. The falsely positive and constantly cheerful clown-mask can be so badly knocked about by the trials of life that it splits and falls off, despite the desperate efforts of the wearer to keep it in place.

"Everything's terrific here! Terrific! No, they're tears of laughter. Can anybody lend me a rope?"

Some people cling onto their mask like a drowning man to a lifebuoy, even after they've reached middle age. Sometimes even they no longer know what is the mask and what is their real self. If you've been going round for thirty years saying: "Feel sorry for me, I need so much pity!" you might well have ended up believing it yourself. "I need lots of pity," one thinks sadly, without having the slightest idea why.

Anyone who has taken to wearing an intellectual mask in the foolishness of youth runs the risk of wearing it for the whole of his life. It's easy for us to become what we think the people we come across expect of us. We are fifty years old and would like to read comics like *Beano, Viz, Playboy-Penny, Cheeky-Chappie*, but that's simply not possible. We are forced to read Yrkdorf Brattenwurst's latest book, *Black Angst Barefoot* in order to live up to the mask we created when we were younger. We think, and we are absolutely right, that *Black Angst Barefoot* is a pretentious, incomprehensible load of old codswallop, but we can't possibly say so. Instead we furrow our intellectual brow and peer with our serious eyes from behind our horn-rimmed spectacles and say: "Brattenwurst has really captured the ephemeral subvalidity of the post-structural scepticism towards logocentricity." And our friends nod in agreement.

Or is it pity?

And so, when you are young and a little uncertain about life, be careful what kind of a mask you wear. One of these days you might be too old to raise the strength to remove it.

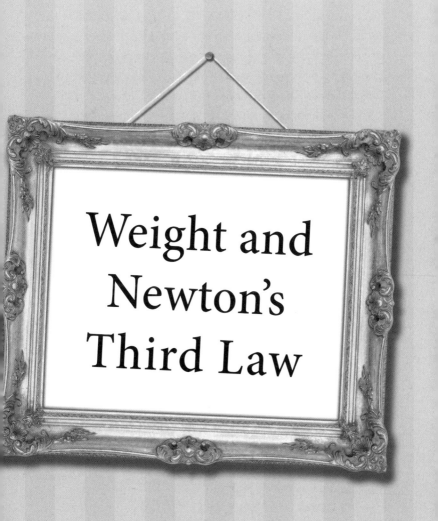

Weight and Newton's Third Law

It's easy to put on a bit of weight as the years go by. It's also more difficult to lose it when you are a bit older. The extra kilos you put on when you're thirty are generally not too difficult to get rid of, but the same kilos are not nearly as easy to lose when you're in your fifties. Your metabolism decreases when you get older, i.e. you don't burn off the calories so easily, which means that if you continue for the whole of your life to eat as much as you did in your twenties, there is a considerable risk that by the age of eighty you will weigh four hundred and sixty kilos.

Do you need to slim when you get older? That depends how much you weigh, of course. Many people keep the same weight all their lives, but it is usual to put on weight. But does it matter if you are a bit too fat? It might not, but being overweight is a risk factor for such ailments as diabetes and heart disease, so it's just as well if you don't weigh as much as a medium-sized hippopotamus. How do you know if you are overweight? If your talking scales burst into tears when you stand on them, you can assume that you weigh too much. If people refuse to travel in a lift with you, that could also be an indication that you weigh more than you should. If you are on a cruise in a biggish ship and the captain asks you always to stay in the middle of the boat, it might be as well to take the hint.

There are also various formulae for working out if you are overweight. You know the kind of thing: take your height in centimetres and multiply it by 0.8. Then divide the result by your weight in kilos times 1.45. Then subtract your waist measurement multiplied by 2.36 and add the length in centimetres of the last pair of trousers you have bought. Add to the result the number of pieces of chocolate (coffee cream) you would like to be eating just now. The figure you end up with is totally worthless. It's better to eat a bit less and exercise a bit more.

But if you do need to lose some kilos because your weight has slowly crept up as the years passed by, what should you do? As everybody knows, there is an infinite number of slimming diets. Slim with carbohydrates, slim without carbohydrates, slim with fat, without fat, with whey-cheese, cabbage soup, the air hostess diet (what do pilots eat?) eggs, red wine, figs or Spanish pepper. You could go to the gym (where all the blokes look like Arnold Schwartzenegger and all the women look like Sylvester Stallone), or you could slim using the Big Water Method (you lose five kilos but gain seven litres). Never a week goes by without some newspaper or other announcing with a fanfare of trumpets a new slimming method with guaranteed results. In practice you can't be sure that these methods will work. You live on salad, tasteless broth and two small potatoes and after a week you have put on one-and-a-half kilos. It's not funny. It can feel bad enough growing old without having to put on weight as well.

It's not just the fact that you tend to put on weight as you grow older, there is also an interesting redistribution of where the kilos go to. They sort of slide down. The law of gravity becomes more evident. Is it the case that gravity increases, the older one gets? That seems to be so. It's not clear if Newton was aware of this – if he was, he ought to have formulated Newton's Third Law: Gravity increases with increasing age. It's easy to see this law working in practice. With increased age, stomachs, breasts and chins are pulled downwards. This must mean that you become more sensitive to the law of gravity, the older you are. This is presumably Newton's fault.

Old at Twenty?

When are you old? In the chapter "How Old Are You?", it was established that age is relative. When we are twenty we think that thirty-year-olds are rather ancient, and when we are forty we think that thirty-year-olds are rather young. All the time, we keep shifting the goalposts with regard to what might be considered old. "Forty isn't all that old," we say when we are thirty-nine-and-a-half. When we were twenty-five we didn't think there was much difference between being forty and being sixty: in both cases those concerned were gaga and should be sitting in some kind of home with a blanket round their knees. When I was in the first term of my medical studies, I was in a lecture sitting next to a female student who whispered in my ear that she thought the lecturer, who was also our tutor, was "really handsome and sexy". She maintained that she wouldn't mind getting together with him "if only he wasn't so bloody old". Our lecturer was aged twenty-eight.

If you have a big enough chip on your shoulder about age, you can feel old at practically any age you like. Lots of people dread their thirtieth birthday: "you're old at thirty"; others can pass forty and fifty without feeling the need to discover where the nearest suicide jump is. When you feel old is an individual thing, as are the reasons for doing so. The differences are both great and paradoxical. There are people who, when they meet and mix with significantly younger people, feel young because all the others around them are young. And there are people who feel extremely old for precisely the same reason. You can feel old (irrespective of your age) when you are reminded of something a few years in the past that you will never be able to repeat. We can only attend a school-leaving party once, we can only celebrate our twenty-fifth birthday once, we can't turn the clock back no matter how hard we try.

The relative view we have of age is illustrated clearly by the American film star Kirk Douglas in part two of his memoirs. In that he writes wistfully about wishing he were young again: "Just imagine being forty-five again! Or sixty-five! Or seventy-five!" You can feel young or old at any age at all.

When you celebrate a "big" birthday, you are often reminded of the fact that you are growing older. The milestones for these birthdays are displayed like big signs along the motorway of life, and the signs seem to be more frequent the older we get. It is obviously completely irrational to think that there is a difference between being forty-nine years and three hundred and sixty-four days old, for instance, and being fifty: but most of us think that way even so. There is something magic about birthdays ending in zero, some scary mysticism about the numbers that is beyond all reason. At birthday parties when the poor birthday child has completed another ten years, a speech has to be delivered about what it feels like to be entering a new age-decade. It doesn't matter how young or how old you are. On your twentieth birthday you are no longer a teenager, on your fortieth you're not so young any more, and when you reach your ninetieth birthday the first candle on your birthday cake has burnt down by the time you have managed to light the last one.

Worst of all is the your fiftieth birthday, when "you're standing on the pinnacle of life" – an ill-concealed euphemism for "it's downhill all the way from here". "Life begins at forty" is another popular birthday cliché, which doesn't work very well when you get to fifty. Delivering a speech and claiming that "life begins at fifty" doesn't sound credible. The birthday child has just been given the sack, heard from his dentist that he needs a new bridge, had an attack of gout and been informed by the Inland Revenue that he has to pay an unexpectedly steep tax bill. If this is "standing on the pinnacle of life", what's it going to be like when you are sixty?

You can also feel old prematurely if you discover that your body isn't quite so hale and hearty as it used to be. This is a discovery you can make rather early on. If you are a ballet dancer or an elite sportsman, you might notice that at thirty you are no longer quite as quick, agile, or lightning-fast to react as you used to be. Old age is creeping up on you and makes its presence felt, and you're thirty-one. A forty-year-old friend who played basketball in his spare time with others of his own age told me that some years back they used to sit around in the dressing room after the match talking about beer and birds. Now they exchanged views on knee injuries and receding hair.

How do you feel when you celebrate a "big" birthday? You often wonder what exactly is involved in completing another ten years, and think back as well as forwards, and sometimes sideways as well. When you reach thirty, if you are a positive person you might think: "Terrific, terrific, terrific! I have the whole of life to look forward to, full of exciting possibilities!" If your personality is slightly different,

you might think on celebrating your thirtieth birthday: "Help! Thirty! No, no, now I'm old. I don't want to be an old codger with a Volvo, a semi-detached house in the suburbs, a mortgage, screaming kids and a monotonous job for the rest of my life. I want to be young and irresponsible and party all round the clock. Thirty! Bloody hell! Does that mean I'm too old to become a rock star now?"

At forty you generally think that you've progressed sufficiently far along the road to preclude the necessity of celebrating: "Forty? It was better being thirty. I wouldn't mind being thirty again. What have I achieved in life so far? Not a lot. I have a pretty awful job and a pretty awful marriage. I ought really to divorce Daphne now and start all over again. It's still not too late. Forty isn't all that old. Not compared to fifty or sixty. There are people who are lively and successful despite he fact that they're old, forty-five or so. My uncle carried on working until he was sixty-eight. Then he dropped down dead. But forty isn't all that much. I don't feel well. Do they really have to put forty candles on the cake? It looks like a bloody torchlight procession!"

When you get to the Big One, the birthday of all birthdays, when you reach fifty, you have every reason to think about the state of affairs: "Fifty. Ah well. Is this all it was? There's nothing special about your fiftieth birthday, in fact. I'm one day older than I was yesterday, that's

nothing to shout about. Tomorrow I'll be another day older still.
– Fifty – It sounds rather a lot, I must say. I suppose one has to be
grateful that not everybody came with crystal glass presents – I told
everybody that I preferred bottles. But Jim and Betty turned up with a
bloody crystal glass vase even so. I can give it to David for his fiftieth
birthday next month. David actually looks much older than I do, even
though he's more than a month younger. I don't like speeches. What
do they mean, the pinnacle of life?! It's a bloody downhill slope. But
it's not all over yet. I'm not all that ancient. Should I marry Sophie?
Or is an age difference of twenty-six years too much? She thought
she might be pregnant the last time I spoke to her. Am I too old to
be a father again? Fifty isn't all that old. Charlie Chaplin and Clint
Eastwood had children when they'd turned sixty. And Harry at the
office has a young family and he's fifty-three. But he's grey in the face
and looks as if he might keel over at any moment. On a day like today
you think about life. How it's been so far and what it might be like
in future. There's something special about celebrating your fiftieth
birthday after all. I'm glad they didn't put any candles on the cake."

And suddenly it's time to be sixty: "Ah well, that's about it. Sixty years
old. Not long to go now. I'll soon be a pensioner. It's amazing how
time flies. It's not long since I celebrated my fiftieth birthday. I really
shouldn't have married Sophie. I'm too old to have little kids running
around. Sixty is not a good age for little kids. Clint Eastwood can afford
nannies, of course. Mind you, he looks worn out even so. But maybe
that's nothing to do with the kids, more to do with all that shooting. I

read in a magazine that he plays golf. Maybe I should take up golf. Or painting china. Perhaps I could combine the two, and paint golf balls. I suppose I ought to have my prostate checked. Bert is only fifty-nine and he has a problem with his prostate. Ah well, I expect it will be OK. I wonder if the crystal glass vase I got from David and Sue was the one I got from Jim and Betty for my fiftieth. It looks exactly the same. It's been doing the rounds, I expect. I wonder if it's the one I saw on Arthur's mantelpiece when he celebrated his sixtieth a couple of years ago. I suppose I could give it to Andrew next year when he's sixty."

Time rolls on inexorably, and before you know where you are it's time to be seventy: "Seventy today. I suppose I'm not all that young any more. I was sixty only the other day, time passes so quickly when you get older. Still, you have to be grateful for being healthy. Well, healthy and *healthy*. The doc says that at my age almost everybody has prostate problems, nothing special about that. The knee is more of a problem. But that's the way it is when you get older, of course. When I was young I was always fit as a fiddle. But it's a long time since I was young. Seventy is quite a lot. My dad lived to be seventy-two. Hmm. It's nice to have a party, a cake and all that. And I've received some lovely presents. I seem to recognize that crystal glass vase. I wonder where I've seen it before."

And if you are lucky, you might celebrate your hundredth birthday: "Terrific, terrific, terrific! I have the whole of life to look forward to, full of exciting possibilities."

If we stay alive and keep healthy, there might well be a little birthday party when we reach eighty as well: "Oh dear! My false teeth are slipping a bit, but the cake tastes good. Cream cake is lovely. And easy to chew. It's not so easy eating a chocolate cake with nuts in. It's nice having a birthday. Eighty is quite a lot. That's a handsome-looking filly over there, I wonder who she is. Maybe I ought to make a move. If I can be bothered. Maybe it's best to stick to the cake. All those little kids are kicking up a hell of a row. How many of them are there? I can't remember seeing as many as this when I celebrated my seventieth. Or was it my sixtieth? But parties are fun. Did I remember to take my medicine this morning? Never mind, a piece of cake will be just as good I expect."

More and more people are celebrating their ninetieth birthday: "Why have they set fire to the table? What? Birthday cake? Is it somebody's birthday? Me, did you say? How old? Ninety? That's amazing. And a cake and all that, wow, great stuff. I remember when I had my fiftieth. Or was it when I was seventy-five? It was great fun anyway. That must be eight to ten years ago now. Boy, that was a party to remember! We had those little gherkins, the ones that are called something in French. Good grief, ninety years old. And presents as well – many thanks. The crystal glass vase is lovely, I used to have one like that when I was young. I suppose I'm not all that young any more now. What kind of a cake is it?"